M000073759

**Knowledge for Sale**

**Infrastructures Series**

edited by Geoffrey C. Bowker and Paul N. Edwards

# Knowledge for Sale

## The Neoliberal Takeover of Higher Education

Lawrence Busch

The MIT Press
Cambridge, Massachusetts
London, England

© 2014 Éditions Quae. © 2017 Massachusetts Institute of Technology, Introduction.

First English language edition published by the MIT Press.

Originally published as *Le marché aux connaissances* by Lawrence Busch, © 2014 Éditions Quae

All rights reserved. No part of this book may be reproduced in any form by any electronic or mechanical means (including photocopying, recording, or information  storage and retrieval) without permission in writing from the publisher.

This book was set in Stone Sans and Stone Serif by Toppan Best-set Premedia Limited. Printed and bound in the United States of America.

Library of Congress Cataloging-in-Publication Data

Names: Busch, Lawrence, author.
Title: Knowledge for sale : the neoliberal takeover of higher education / Lawrence Busch.
Description: Cambridge, MA : The MIT Press, 2017. | Series: Infrastructures series | Includes bibliographical references and index.
Identifiers: LCCN 2016031906 | ISBN 9780262036078 (hardcover : alk. paper)
Subjects: LCSH: Education, Higher--Economic aspects. | Education, Higher--Aims and objectives. | Universities and colleges--Administration. | Neoliberalism. | Capitalism and education.
Classification: LCC LC67.6 .B87 2017 | DDC 338.43378--dc23 LC record available at https://lccn.loc.gov/2016031906

10  9  8  7  6  5  4  3  2  1

To the memory of Susan Leigh Star, mentor and friend

VSNixson

" Five full years of collecting specimens and another year for analysis?  But without at least three published articles by next year, you will lose your university position, Mr. Darwin!"

# Contents

# Preface to the English Language Edition

It is perhaps all too widely believed that scholarly knowledge emerges from the lonely work of *individual* scholars who dig through libraries and archives, engage in all sorts of experiments, examine physical objects left to us by the past, analyze statistical data, or engage in myriad other tasks. Similarly, others believe that knowledge is transferred from one person or generation to another intact. However, a few moments reflection should make clear that knowledge generation and its transfer to another generation as well as to those outside the university community is a far more complex process.

Let's begin with the production of knowledge through research and scholarship.[1] As anyone who has visited a research university[2] or research institute immediately observes, the production of knowledge requires a vast physical infrastructure. That infrastructure includes the myriad libraries, offices, laboratories, research centers, computers, and all that is necessary to research. Maintenance of that infrastructure is a huge enterprise, including the financial and other record keeping essential to administration of research, but also the furnishing of electricity, water, scientific equipment, scholarly journals, office supplies, computer centers, and the like. Each of these services requires the work of numerous persons who build, maintain, and replace parts of that infrastructure. Each of those persons must have at least a minimal level of competence in whatever tasks they perform.

All of this, in turn, is quite useless without nearly continuous interaction among scholars, technicians, and staff who compare notes, debate options, determine strategies, invent new products and processes—who engage in research in the literal sense (i.e., they search again and re-enact their fields of inquiry). Put differently, all the various actors—from scholars and secretaries to electricians to janitors—must perform their tasks using the appropriate material objects at their disposal. Only then can they create, transfer, revise, and challenge—in a word, enact—knowledge.

In short, the production of knowledge requires a vast and increasingly international network of persons *and* things, a sociotechnical infrastructure if you wish. That infrastructure—if it works as expected—is usually invisible to those who inhabit it. It is not that I don't see the hallways through which I walk to reach my office. It is that as long as the infrastructure works as I have come to expect, I pay little attention to it. I only notice it when the heat is off in the winter, when there are no paperclips, when the computer system is down.

Conversely, during my career I have visited numerous universities and research institutes in so-called developing nations in which apparently well-trained scholars and scientists lacked one or more facets of sociotechnical infrastructure. As a result, they were incapable of participating in scholarship. A few examples should suffice to emphasize this point. In many instances, I arrived at a research facility to be greeted by scientists with doctoral degrees from excellent American, French, or British universities. I was shown around the laboratories, which were eerily quiet. Why? Because the scientific instruments were in disrepair and no technicians and/or spare parts were available, because the labor required to plant and harvest an experimental crop was unavailable at the critical time, because the steady supply of electrical current necessary to run delicate instruments or some other aspect of the infrastructure was lacking. Similarly, I have visited universities and research institutes that, owing to a lack of funds, had received no new scholarly journals for a decade or more. Equally problematic is the well-equipped research institute or university with poorly trained or nonexistent staff.

In contrast, on one visit to China where this issue is well understood, I visited a busy laboratory in an inland research facility where a large number of technicians were busy operating several chromatographs. I asked what they did when these delicate and complex machines broke down. They answered that a manufacturer's representative was available just a short distance from the lab and could be easily reached by phone.

What I have just recounted with respect to research is also the case for education. As with research, education requires a sociotechnical infrastructure to be effective. In most instances, students do not arrive at universities with precise agendas outlining what they want to learn. Were that to be the case, there would be no need for education. Instead, effective education opens new avenues to knowledge for students, allows them to question the accepted wisdom, challenges what they thought was obvious. Indeed, education does not involve the transfer of knowledge but rather its translation (Latour 2005). That is to say, the transfer metaphor suggests that a source (the teacher) sends a message to a receiver (a student). This is followed by some sort of feedback (a test) that determines whether the signal was received. In contrast, a translation metaphor emphasizes that effective learning requires that (1) the receiver translate the message into terms that she can understand, (2) the communication is multidirectional or dialogical (i.e., that the sender and receiver are part of a learning community), and (3) the end result of successful education is that all parties learn.

Of late, in an effort to reduce the cost of education, many universities have developed Massive Open Online Courses (MOOCs) and other means of broadcasting lectures to all who are connected to the Internet. (A century ago, they tried the same thing with correspondence courses and later with radio and educational television.) At the same time, others have demanded the use of standardized tests to provide feedback on whether learning has been successful. I shall have more to say about the limits to this approach later in this book. What I wish to bring to your attention here is that all means of communicating knowledge require a sociotechnical infrastructure. This infrastructure includes some combination of classrooms, blackboards, chalk, pencils, pens, paper, audiovisual technologies, computers, and other material objects as well as teachers, students, and staff. These persons and things must be organized into a coherent infrastructure such that attention is paid to learning rather than to the nonfunctional projector, the absent teacher, or the inadequate classroom. In summary, as with research, education also requires an organized sociotechnical infrastructure that performs sufficiently seamlessly that it is largely unnoticed.

What I just noted about research and education is equally relevant to links between the university and the larger community. Although the methods of reaching audiences beyond enrolled students may vary, including, for example, the many bulletins providing advice to farmers issued by agricultural extension services, visits to off-campus sites and short courses, in each instance a sociotechnical infrastructure is necessary to translate the knowledge found at the university into forms useful to other audiences. As with teaching and research, that infrastructure must be nearly invisible to be effective.

But this is not all. Every contemporary society also designs and redesigns the infrastructures that permit the production and reproduction of knowledge. These infrastructures are not merely empty containers that might be filled with any sort of knowledge. They are constructed, enacted in such a manner as to promote certain outcomes and discourage others. On a most obvious level, few universities have a department of astrology; that field of study is generally not deemed worthy of university infrastructure. Similarly, the US National Science Foundation has been directed by Congress to support some fields of research with great largesse while providing little or no funds to other fields. Over time, these and other aspects of infrastructure have changed markedly, but because infrastructure is largely invisible and change is often slow, it is not easy to recognize. However, of late there have been numerous attempts to change, transform, and re-enact the knowledge infrastructure in rather radical ways.

Consider that recently Japan's Ministry of Education announced that it would eliminate humanities and social science programs from public universities. There was considerable uproar about this, followed by a claim by the Ministry that they were misunderstood. However, although the Ministry backed down, there is little question as to what they proposed. This is but one example of the attempts in numerous nations to redefine the knowledge infrastructure. I discuss many other such attempts—some more successful than others—to transform knowledge infrastructures in this volume. One might summarize the position taken by those who wish to alter the extant infrastructure as an argument that the only knowledge worth pursuing is that which has more or less immediate market value. Knowledge that creates educated citizens, allows us to better make sense of our place in the world, introduces students to critical thinking, allows us to better understand the past, inspires enthusiasm in the quest for more knowledge, and promotes new practices that do not have direct market value are at best to be downgraded. At the limit, as the Japanese Ministry of Education attempted, they are to be eliminated.

As I argue in more detail below, this transformation of the knowledge infrastructure developed in large part from brilliant but ultimately flawed work by several economists, including F. A. Hayek (1973–1979), Milton Friedman (2002 [1962]), Gary Becker (1997), and James Buchanan (2003). It is what Angus Burgin (2012) has called *The Great Persuasion*. They provided a rationale for reorganizing society as a whole, including higher education and research, to meet the needs of the market. Their followers, including politicians across the spectrum as well as a significant portion of the business community, began yet ongoing work to transform the knowledge infrastructure so as to make it more market-like in the belief that in so doing they would produce a better society. Hence, a wide range of changes have been instituted around the world by political leaders who have little else in common. Nations as diverse as China, the United States, France, and Pakistan have all embraced aspects of this perspective and made more or less successful changes in the knowledge infrastructure (see e.g., Harvey 2005). Nations such as Chile and Iraq have had it foisted on them (Klein 2007).

Among the market-like changes they have instituted (in varying degrees) are (1) shifting the cost of education from the State to individual students, (2) redefining higher education as a search for the highest pay job, (3) turning scholarly research into an individualized form of competition based on a wide range of metrics (e.g., numbers of citations, the value of grants, the numbers of patents), (4) instituting national and global competitions among universities and research institutes for funding and prestige, and (5) increasing the numbers and enhancing the power and salaries of administrators in return for pursuing these market-like objectives. Together these market-like changes have transformed the self-understanding and consequent behavior of students, scholars, and administrators. Far too frequently we tend to think of ourselves in market terms and act on market signals.

Of course, these changes have neither occurred all at once nor been implemented in the same way everywhere. In addition, they have met with varying degrees of resistance by students, faculty, staff, and the general public. But together they have changed the knowledge infrastructure such that market-like terminology is now commonplace in higher education and research. Talk of return on investment, "incentivizing" faculty and students, value added, and other terms once reserved for the business community have become part of the daily discussions in higher education and research. Moreover, these terms have become grounds for acting. Put differently, they have led to the enacting of a different kind of university and research institute.

They have done so with little or no discussion among those affected or the public at large. This volume is designed to help correct that omission, to open these changes to democratic debate before they succeed in cutting off democratic debate entirely.

Lawrence Busch, June 2016

## Acknowledgments

This volume had its origin in a request by the "Sciences en Questions" Work Group founded at the Institut National de la Recherche Agronomique (INRA) in 1994. I was asked to write it by Dr. Paul Robin on behalf of the group. I would like to thank both Dr. Robin as well as the other members of the group for giving me this opportunity. Moreover, Dr. Raphael Larrère pored over both the English and French versions, suggesting numerous improvements. His commentaries helped to strengthen the manuscript. In addition, a small grant from the Fondation Agropolis allowed me to spend three enjoyable months in Montpellier, France, where, among other things, I put the finishing touches on this manuscript. Furthermore, I would like to thank the anonymous reviewers of the English language edition as well as Dr. Geof Bowker, who read and commented on the introduction to the English language edition, and Katie Helke of the MIT Press, who shepherded the manuscript through the review process. Note that any texts not available in English were translated from the original French by me. Of course, I take full responsibility for any errors of omission or commission herein.

# The Market for Knowledge

The last 30 years have been marked by a profound transformation of the sciences, liberal arts, public universities, and research institutions. Although the details have varied considerably from nation to nation, the general directions of change are remarkably similar. In particular, there has been an increase in emphasis on market-like competition—among institutions, scientists, scholars, and students. Concomitant with increased competition, there has also been an increased emphasis on audits. Numerous questions have been posed about their performance including: Have university rankings improved? Have graduation rates increased? Have students moved quickly through the program? Have faculty published more articles in top journals? Moreover, based on the audit, what should be done? Should those who have done well be rewarded? Should those who have done poorly be reorganized or subject to additional audits?

Considerable effort has been expended in attempts to answer these and related questions. Although there has been substantial resistance to the changes, much of it has come to naught. Instead, there has been a marked shift in faculty behavior, valuing publications above education and public engagement.

Confident in their belief in a market world, politicians and government officials have been able to transform institutions, persons, and what counts as knowledge in the process.

In this volume, I attempt to trace the links between the performances of a particular version of economic science known as "neoliberalism" and the restructuring of universities and research institutes. First, I note the multiple crises that face virtually everyone on earth—crises that higher education and research must address. Then I show how economic science has been performed so as to alter the ways in which public research, education, and engagement are undertaken and measured. I contrast that with my own position in this complex and ongoing debate. I follow that by explaining in detail the transformations that have occurred in administration, education, research, and public engagement, respectively. I pay particular attention to the paths not taken and conclude by asking: For whom and for what do we want knowledge? What kind of future society do we desire? How might we get there? Let me begin by describing some of the crises.

# Crises

The shifts in higher education and research would be of relatively minor import were it not for the major crises facing the world today. Among them we can count climate change, food price volatility, water shortages, rising energy costs, widespread obesity, and, last but not least, the financial crisis—not to mention wars, racism, and poverty. Each of these is a wicked problem (Rittel and Webber 1973) that cannot be solved through straightforward puzzle solving. This is the case because (1) each involves not only technical change but iterative changes in norms, laws, and standards; and (2) each crisis is intertwined with the others. Moreover, grappling with these problems is not only a necessity for us, it is essential for future generations. Let us briefly consider each of them.

**Climate change.** Despite some who continue to doubt it, not only is climate change upon us, but it is almost certainly the result of human activities. However, regardless of responsibility, climate change will require measures that go far beyond the market. Although there have been some well-intentioned attempts to mitigate climate change through, for example, the Kyoto Protocols, the overall effects have been minimal. The biggest producers of greenhouse gases did not sign on, and the protocols have been all too easy to manipulate. More important, even the best market-based climate change policies to date suffer from three major flaws: First, future generations have no voice in market-based decision making, although they will be most affected by decisions made today. Second, regardless of any attempts at mitigation, coastal plains—where many of the world's largest cities are located—will likely be flooded as the oceans rise. Decisions will have to be made in numerous locales about whether to resettle populations or attempt to build dykes. These decisions will have to be made by governments, and they are best made before major flooding occurs. Third, research needs to be undertaken now to determine what technologies will be effective in what locales; such research is unlikely to be undertaken by the private sector as the risks of failure are high. The usefulness of those technologies will be in large part a function of the policies enacted by governments.

**Rising and more volatile food prices.** Food is not merely a desire but rather a basic human necessity. Hence, although one can decide to avoid television and computers, one cannot stop eating. There are essentially three options. First, one can grow food oneself, which assumes that one has access to land and the required skills; given the rapid urbanization of the world, this is impossible for most people. Second, one can purchase food in the market, as most of us do; this, of course, requires that one have the ready cash. Third, in desperate circumstances, one can steal food so as to survive. What this means is that rising food prices, although of minor consequence for most of us in the rich world, are of central concern to the poor. In some nations, we have already seen food riots.

Moreover, in recent years, food prices have risen substantially and become more volatile, even as *there is sufficient food produced in the world to feed everyone* (Hossein, King, and Kelbert 2013). Volatility has increased because a significant amount of cropland is now devoted to fuel production. In addition, in some nations such as the United States, futures markets for crops have been opened to speculators who have no intention of ever taking delivery of the crop in question. Furthermore, productivity growth has leveled off in many nations, in part a result of more erratic weather conditions. Grappling with this complex set of relations among food prices, climate change, and the need for transport fuels requires research that cuts across disciplinary boundaries and is both social and technical in nature; it is sociotechnical.

**Water shortages.** Like food, we all need water. Yet water for agriculture, manufacturing, and domestic use is likely to be in short supply. Already, in some parts of the world, there are disputes over water use. In some instances, these disputes are between farmers and city dwellers; in other places they are between nations that depend on a single river (e.g., the Nile). As with food, there have been riots over water prices in some nations. We cannot afford to "let the market decide" about water use because the market will only register effective demand. Put differently, we cannot let those with the most money determine how water will be used because to do so is to consign those without monetary means to a life that is "nasty, brutish and short," as Hobbes would have put it.

**Rising energy costs.** Energy costs are rising everywhere in part as a result of the growth of manufacturing and rising incomes among the middle and upper classes in India and China, among other places. They demand more energy and look to industrialized nations for the "good life." In addition, there is little cheap oil left, forcing oil companies to shift to more costly sources (both in monetary and energy values). Furthermore, as the environmental costs of coal production have become better understood, most nations are trying to reduce reliance on coal. Hence, oil shale and bituminous sands are currently being developed as energy sources. They are fraught with controversy as they pose a number of environmental problems. Both require considerable use of water and risk contaminating local water supplies, while mining bituminous sands also involves removing vegetation from large areas. Moreover, given that the environmental costs are undervalued and not adequately taken into account by many markets, we cannot rely on markets to resolve these issues.*

**Widespread obesity.** Obesity is on the rise globally, among both the rich and the poor. Doubtless, the rise in obesity is related to a change in diet—toward the cheap fat-, salt-, and sugar-rich diet successfully marketed by many large food companies—and our increasingly urban, sedentary lives. It is also linked to (often hidden) subsidies for the production of maize that make it an ingredient in countless products either as carbohydrate or sugar. Obesity has a wide range of health problems associated with it, most of which raise healthcare costs. Moreover, a small industry has developed attempting to grapple with the causes and consequences of obesity. Here there is little question that the market

* NB: When I originally wrote this book, energy prices were soaring. Of late, they have declined, although there is some evidence to suggest that they are rising again. However, low prices for fossil fuel-based energy present the same, if not greater, environment problems. They also put price pressure on alternative energy sources. — LB.

*is* the problem. Unless the terms of food marketing are changed (e.g., by removing subsidies and taxing high-sugar products), the market will continue to provide perverse incentives to all of us.

**Financial crises.** After the Great Depression, considerable effort was made to ensure that finance was adequately regulated, such that in the future it would not drag the global economy down again. However, starting in the 1980s, much of that regulation was relaxed or repealed. I need not go into the details here because virtually everyone reading this has been personally affected by the massive bailouts to failing banks, the collapse of the housing markets in several nations, the austerity imposed within the European Union, and the painfully slow improvements since. That said, while fighting against further regulation, the financial sector recovered rapidly, paying bonuses to its executives while the rest of us faced declining real wages and wealth. Even now, some years later, we are discovering that a wide range of unethical and often illegal behavior has been all too common in finance, ranging from the fixing of interbank rates to the failure to inform investors of risks. Importantly, although the financial crisis was due almost entirely to the actions of financial institutions, only a handful of persons have been convicted of crimes, and only a few fines have been levied. Instead, national governments have inherited the bill. We are all paying for their behavior through higher taxes and/or declining public services, whereas those responsible remain unscathed.

\*\*\*

There is no single formula, permanent set of policies and practices, or fixed marker of success in these intertwined endeavors.

Nor can these endeavors be merely parceled out to individual technical disciplines. They require interdisciplinary projects and programs that include both persons with technical expertise in many fields of science and engineering as well as those with competence in the humanities, law, and social sciences. Put differently, building more sustainable societies—even defining sustainability—will require changes to both our practices and our imaginaries. Because we can never begin again *de novo*, this will have to be accomplished in an iterative fashion. What we desire will be a function of both our collective goals and our collective practices; both will change as they interact with each other.

Importantly, these crises are not likely to be mitigated by market means for several reasons. First, they fail to consider those who cannot participate in the market. Future generations and those lacking the wherewithal to participate in markets have no voice in how we address these issues, but both groups will most certainly feel the consequences.

Second, they demand social improvements, not individual ones. Although I might well reduce the amount of energy I use, maximize the environmentally friendly ways in which I live, avoid high-fat and high-sugar foods, reduce my carbon emissions by using public transport, invest my money conservatively, and install water-saving devices on my faucets, my individual actions are simply insufficient because there are millions of people who are unlikely to do any of those things unless institutional changes are made.

Third, the market logic of supply and demand is inadequate. Each of these crises is not independent of the others. The financial, climate, and energy crises affect the food supply. Water shortages affect our ability to produce energy and food. Market incentives in our food system promote diets that create obesity, thereby putting extra demands on medical institutions. In short, these are wicked problems—problems that admit no simple "solution." New knowledge will be central in addressing each of these issues. However, we will require not only the creation of new technologies but also a questioning of our values and a transformation of the skills required of nearly everyone. In particular, creativity, teamwork, and critical thinking will become far more important (Anderson and Rainie 2012). We will need to understand how to give the public voice in determining how to proceed under conditions of both uncertainty and complexity. We will need to develop new policies, laws, standards, and technologies. Higher education and research can and must play a key role in addressing these issues. To do so, we will need to rethink and re-enact both. We will need to transform research and education. But before turning to these challenges, let me first try to portray the central tenets of neoliberalism. As you will see, neoliberalism occupies a central, although sometimes invisible, role in our dilemma.

## Liberalisms and Neoliberalisms

Since the end of World War II and especially since the collapse of the Soviet Bloc in the late 1980s, governments around the world have embraced markets and market-like competitions. We have been told that the market is the solution to both political and economic problems as well as—and arguably more importantly—the source of individual liberty (e.g., Becker and Becker 1997; Friedman 2002 [1962]; Hayek 2007 [1944]). This transformation to the (quasi)market-based governance of all institutions—including universities and research institutes, but also health care, policing, social work, and other institutions—was initially labeled "neoliberalism" by its supporters, although in recent years they have only reluctantly used that label.

Some persons consider neoliberalism as a school of thought in the discipline of economics. Others consider it to be a program of action. Still others consider it an ideology. To some degree it is all three. As Mirowski (2009) argues, neoliberalism can be understood as a "thought collective" because it does not consist of a single, clearly stated doctrine cast in stone, but rather an ongoing debate among its supporters promoted through the Mont Pelerin Society (2009) and various neoliberal think tanks. Neoliberalism is also a social movement in that its supporters have successfully sought and largely succeeded in transforming much of the world—although differently in different places—over the last 30 to 40 years. Finally, neoliberalism can be considered an ideology, as evidenced by the abiding faith among many politicians, business leaders, and members of the general public in the primacy of markets and competition.

Classical liberalism from which neoliberalism springs is (as the word implies) linked with liberty, but because the full liberty of one person would restrict the liberty of others, liberals are agreed that some form of constraint is necessary to optimize the liberty of all. From its inception, this posed a dilemma for liberals. On the one hand, they embraced the notion of *laissez-faire*, believing that markets were natural and would work to benefit all if only the State did not intervene and market actors were at liberty to conduct their business as they saw fit. As Hobbes (1651, 133) put it, "The greatest Liberty of Subjects dependeth on the Silence of the Law." On the other hand, they realized that the State was necessary to both protect participants in the market through contract, tort, and anti-fraud law and ensure various freedoms such as those of speech, association, and religion. As a result of these two different aspects of liberty, the term is ambiguous, as is the notion of liberalism. Moreover, given the diverse histories of various nations, liberalism often divides along national lines.

French liberalism, found in the works of Montesquieu, Voltaire, and Constant among others, desires that limits be put on the power of the State so as to be able to speak and act freely; this version of liberalism is amenable to a *laissez-faire* position. In contrast, however, another strand of French liberalism emphasizes the role of the State in *promoting* liberty; to a great extent, this was the rallying cry of the French Revolution. Both have been present through much of French history. They remain present in the current debates over equality in higher education.

Much the same division can be found in American liberalism. As noted some years ago, the American Constitution's "due process" clause enacted the civil government of John Locke (Schlatter 1951). That government was to be minimal, embrace *laissez-faire*, and guarantee the liberties of citizens. But some centuries later, in the midst of the Great Depression, Americans embraced a notion of liberalism defined by a large state that intervened in many aspects of daily life so as to ensure that Americans enjoyed freedom from hunger and want among other things. Hence, contemporary American liberals often look to the State to resolve contemporary ills even as they value individual liberties.

Neoliberalism departs from both the *laissez-faire* and statist versions of classical liberalism.[1] On the one hand, neoliberals reject *laissez-faire* approaches, arguing instead that the State must actively intervene to transform institutions into markets and competitive quasi-markets. On the other hand, neoliberals wish to see States limited largely to the rule of law (i.e., to blindly promoting markets and market-like competitions), rather than actively planning and intervening in society. The process of promoting markets and competitions is thus seen as an apolitical, technical task. Not surprisingly, as we shall see, these two starting points create a number of contradictions for both neoliberal theorists and neoliberal societies.

Neoliberalism has its roots in the crises of capitalism during the Great Depression. It can (arguably) be said to have begun at an invitational colloquium in 1938 in Paris. Organized around Walter Lippmann's (1938) *The Good Society* by philosopher of mathematics and logic Louis Rougier, it brought together a significant number of liberal intellectuals and businessmen of the day. Participants included, among others, Austrian economists F. A. Hayek and his mentor Ludwig von Mises, and Lippmann himself. The participants were (rightly!) worried about the rise of various authoritarian States: Nazism in Germany, fascism in Spain and Italy, and communism in the Soviet Union. But they were also concerned about the growth of the State in the United States, France, and Britain. As they saw it, the entire world was drifting down the slippery slope toward authoritarian if not totalitarian regimes.

Moreover, to the participants, classical liberalism appeared utterly inadequate to the job of countering these decidedly illiberal trends. What was needed, as Rougier made clear in his remarks, was a new liberalism, a *"néo-libéralisme"* (Rougier 1939b), that would go beyond the *laissez-faire* approach developed in the 18th century and provide a "Road Code" for bringing the Good Society into being (Rougier 1939a). Although plans were made for the creation of a center to study these issues, war soon intervened. Paris was occupied by the Nazis, and the participants at the Colloquium were scattered. Hence, only after the end of the war did neoliberals begin to organize effectively.

Of particular importance was Hayek's publication of *The Road to Serfdom* in 1944 [2007]. Initially serialized in *Readers Digest*, the volume was particularly well received in the United States. Its publication attracted the attention of several wealthy businessmen who were happy to promote Hayek's ideas. With their support, in 1947, Hayek was able to organize the first postwar meeting of the neoliberals in Switzerland, where they founded the Mont Pelerin Society. Although there was much dispute among the participants and the entire enterprise initially seemed doomed to collapse, continued support from American benefactors combined with a research home at the University of Chicago law school created a core group of supporters who promoted neoliberal perspectives on economics and law (Horn and Mirowski 2009). As noted above, neoliberals do not agree on everything. However, we can briefly summarize some of the generally accepted tenets of neoliberalism today as follows.

**Human knowledge is always limited**. Hence, no person, organization, or government can know enough to plan adequately. In contrast, the free market price mechanism (or its equivalent) provides a means of producing knowledge on which both producers and consumers can act confidently at the same time as it ensures efficiency in the production, distribution, and consumption of goods and services. Hence, if the cost of a new book is high, I may decide to purchase a used one or forego the purchase entirely. In contrast, if the price of a new book is low, I may decide to purchase a new one instead of one that has been used. Book prices may be high because the publisher did not print sufficient copies or the cost of making paper has risen due to a shortage of pulpwood. Whatever the reason(s) may be, I need not know them to make my decision. Moreover, the same price signals apply to producers. Hence, if book prices are high relative to cost, publishers will be spurred on to produce more books; conversely, if book prices are low, publishers will have an incentive to reduce production. Unlike central planning, in which under- or overproduction is always a problem, neoliberals claim that free markets always provide the right signals to producers and consumers.

**An irrefutable logical model can transcend the limits of human knowledge**. Neoliberals argue that, unlike other knowledge, prices in a free market are not based on the knowledge of individual human beings but on logical and mathematical knowledge that is true by definition. Indeed, it is not even amenable to empirical verification. As Hayek (1943, 11) put it, "All that the theory of the social sciences attempts is to provide a technique of reasoning which assists us in connecting individual facts, but which, like logic or mathematics, is not about the facts. It can, therefore..., never be verified or falsified by reference to facts."

In short, from a neoliberal perspective, knowledge of prices in a free market is much like knowledge of geometry. If you claim that you have a triangle the interior angles of which sum to 179°, I would simply reply that you do not have a triangle. A triangle is—*by definition*—a three-sided object whose interior angles sum to 180°. For neoliberals, so it is with free markets (Friedman 2002 [1962]). One might argue that this assertion allows neoliberals to have their cake and eat it, too. On the one hand, they claim that free markets are "natural," in that conformity to the logical model always produces the desired outcomes. But they also argue for a "positive program" for *laissez-faire* (Simons 1948 [1934]), rejecting the older liberal shibboleth that markets will "naturally" spring up wherever the State withdraws. Thus, even as their policies differ from place to place and situation to situation, they share a commitment to making a single order of worth, the market, predominant in all settings, arguing that the market order is the best—and only—route to liberty.

In the name of the market, neoliberals have intervened (1) institutionally (e.g., changing legal statutes), (2) individually (e.g., changing key administrators), and (3) by changing things (e.g., new technologies). Hence, markets and market-like competitions have replaced direct government intervention in promoting higher education and research. At the same time, a variety of legal requirements, bureaucratic rules, and audit mechanisms have been put in place to promote compliance (and sanction noncompliance) with the new market-like rules.

**Institutions must be reshaped so as to fit the logical model.** All government agencies, research and educational institutions, private voluntary organizations, and other institutions must be reconfigured and reshaped as markets and quasi-markets. In practice, this has been accomplished in two complementary ways: introducing commercial practices into all public institutions and opening these institutions to privatization or direct competition from the private sector. This is quite different from the liberals of the 18th and 19th centuries, who argued that the State should merely leave the market alone. In contrast, neoliberals argue that nation-states should be actively involved in the formation of markets and competitions. For the neoliberals, doing so will provide the signals necessary for people to exercise their liberty to make informed choices.

Of course, turning institutions into markets and competitions means simultaneously that other forms of social organization must be diminished or eliminated. Hence, government planning that sends the "wrong" signals to markets must be eliminated. Government subsidies, tariffs, and quotas must be eliminated for the same reasons. In addition, government services must be contracted out whenever possible because it is alleged that this will ensure that those services will be provided in the most efficient ways. Choice must be promoted insofar as possible in all government programs so that individual liberty is expanded.

**The ability of States to intervene in markets must be limited.** International organizations must be created or transformed, including the World Trade Organization, the World Bank, the

International Monetary Fund, and the World Intellectual Property Organization. These organizations serve to limit the market-interfering actions of nation-states even as they promote the creation of global markets in goods and services.

**Social justice as both a concept and a set of policies is rejected as a mirage**. From Hayek's (1976) point of view, it is simply too vague a concept either for use in court decisions or in positive law. As a consequence, "freedom *to*" is promoted whereas "freedom *from*" is ignored or denied. One has the freedom *to* purchase an increasingly wide range of goods and services (if one has the means to do so), but one can never be sure to be free *from* poverty or hunger.

**Selves are to be reconstructed as isolated and entrepreneurial**. The 17th century answer to the question "How is society possible?" was developed by the social contract theorists who assumed that individuals were autonomous. Economists adopted this position as a method of research in the 19th century. It has been made real by (1) turning institutions into markets in which we must make myriad choices *as if* we were autonomous individuals, (2) demanding that each of us makes endless calculations and investments (of money, but also of time, commitment, etc.) to secure our individual future, and (3) redefining all human action as instances of the use of human capital (i.e., as *capital investments in one's personal future*). In short, "[o]n the one hand, (neo)liberal government respects the formal freedom and autonomy of subjects. On the other hand, it governs within and through those independent actions by promoting the very disciplinary technologies deemed necessary for a successful autonomous life" (Langley 2007, 72).

Furthermore, in all organizations, including universities and research institutes, there are those persons who either do the bare minimum to receive a paycheck and/or engage in activities largely unrelated to the organization's goals. Such persons reduce the overall efficiency and effectiveness of the organization. However, because neoliberals see individuals as autonomous rational actors who invest their human capital only as necessary, they assume that *all* those employed in organizations *merely* wish to maximize their own goals and "utilities" and not those of their employer.[2] For the neoliberals, this situation creates a "moral hazard" for the public sector. Any broader civic goals are dismissed as mere propaganda for a given profession.

The "solution" to this problem is to be found in codified form in New Public Management (NPM). Public employees are seen to use public funds to further their own ends, rather than those of the public agency that employs them. As two German supporters of this approach assert:

The NPM approach ... tries to restore operational flexibility, while, at the same time, it tries to limit moral hazard problems. This is done by giving financial autonomy to universities and chairs but also increasing hierarchical self-control, i.e. by increasing the power of deans, chancellors and other internal management positions, as well as competitive elements such as an indicator based performance-dependent resource allocation, evaluations or higher dependence on third-party funds. This leads to the NPM parole of "More autonomy, more hierarchy and more competition." (Schubert and Schmoch 2010, 4–5)

It should be underlined that the fondness for audits is the flip side of competition. Competitions cannot occur unless everyone follows the same rules. Thus, to establish markets and market-like competitions, neoliberal governments must establish rules. These go far beyond the conventional understanding of markets as governed by contract, corporate, property, and anti-fraud laws. Those laws (usually correctly) assume that participants in the market will be relatively independent entities who must be governed by rules that define the competition irrespective of what is to be traded. However, the qualities of goods and services, the degree to which those goods and services are differentiated from others, much of the internal dynamics of the organization, and, most important, the pricing of those goods and services are determined by the competitors in light of market conditions (i.e., the prices at which competitors are selling their goods and services and the willingness of potential consumers to purchase such goods and services). In contrast, paradoxically, NPM imposes a new disciplinary structure for universities in which participation in competitions is mandatory for promoting freedom and responding to the needs of the market.

Furthermore, because neoliberalism has been enacted differently in different places, it is perhaps better to talk of the widespread acceptance of *neoliberalisms* by national elites and considerable segments of the general public in a wide variety of nations, as well as imposition by force in nations such as Chile and Iraq (Klein 2007). This has transformed to some degree virtually all the major institutions of contemporary societies from health services to road and rail infrastructure to government bureaucracies to prison management. However, as I show below, attempting to turn all institutions into markets and competitions degrades discourse while undermining research, education, public engagement, and, ultimately, democracy.

# Beyond Neoliberalisms

Having described the central tenets of neoliberalisms, I need to make clear what my own views are of the goals and values that should be embedded in higher education and research. Like the neoliberals, I believe that liberty is a worthwhile objective, but I find their definition rather limiting. Let me begin with the self.

**The self is social.** As infants we learn who we are through interactions with others. We have no choice in the matter. There is no way to produce selves that are completely free of the influence of others because our selves are fundamentally social (Mead 1913; Thévenot 2006). We are neither the autonomous beings posited by neoliberals and their forebears, Locke and Hobbes, nor fully socialized beings; we are between autonomy and sociality (Rasmussen 1973). Those persons who, by some terrible accident, grow up with little or no contact with others do not become fully human. Moreover, all the institutions of society—from families to schools to religious organizations to workplaces to the military—as well as technologies and the natural world are part of the self-creation process.

**Each institution promotes certain kinds of selves and rejects other kinds.** As children we accept self-production uncritically. Hence, people do not determine for themselves what their mother tongue will be, in which family they shall reside, who their relatives will be, in what kind of society they shall live, and what values they shall hold dear. It is only on reaching adulthood that we become (at least partially) aware of other options, other ways in which we might shape our selves. Even then, that often occurs by chance. We meet someone who challenges our received beliefs. We witness an event that forces us to question the conventional wisdom. We read something that illustrates the falsity of a given closely held belief. Universities, when they do their job best, are particularly effective in this respect. They offer students the opportunity not merely to learn new skills, but to begin to think and act critically about each and every aspect of the social world. Students may decide that the world in which they are comfortable is the right one for them, but they may also decide to change that world, to attempt to modify it in some way or another.

During the heyday of the Soviet Union, much effort was given to molding citizens such that their selves would support the State. The Stakhanovite worker who allegedly produced at a rate several times greater than that of coworkers was glorified as unselfishly giving all to the State. University education focused not on critical thinking, but on turning out scientists and (especially) engineers who would increase the productivity of the Soviet State. They would help the Soviet Union to "catch up" with the capitalist industrial world. Courses on Marxist-Leninist orthodoxy were mandatory; criticism of that orthodoxy brought swift punishment.

In contrast, more recently, especially in the post-Cold War period, much effort has been expended to mold people into risk takers who could and would become ideal participants in a market society. Welfare programs have been cut as unnecessary and undesirable promotions of the "nanny State." Courses on entrepreneurial orthodoxy have become commonplace. Science and engineering research have been promoted not because of the discoveries and inventions that they might produce, but because they might bring increased efficiency, productivity, and profits.

But this is merely the mirror image of the Soviet State. If liberty is what we wish to achieve, it cannot be done by fostering the creation of selves who fit into any predetermined mold. Liberty and freedom require that (1) we encourage people to become reflexively aware of the way that others—as individuals and collectivities—influence their own self-formation, (2) people have the ability to decide—within the limits of social life—what kinds of selves they want to have, and (3) people have the wherewithal to change their selves over the course of their lives. Each of these three aspects of self-formation is appropriately pursued in the context of a university or research institute.

**People, institutions, and things make society together.** In each area of social life, we find institutions, people, and things. Hence, I might recognize the *Institut Nationale de la Recherche Agronomique* by (1) virtue of meeting with its director or one of the many scientists in its employ, (2) the large sign in front of its headquarters, or (3) examining its organizational structure, conventions, or legal standing. Some have emphasized that institutions are made by people, whereas others have argued that institutions make people in a certain fashion. Still others

have argued that things make people and institutions. Yet each
of these unidirectional explanations is lacking; each is much
like asking whether the chicken or the egg came first. In point
of fact, institutions, people, and things all make each other
simultaneously.

**Communities of scholars and invisible colleges are essential
to the creation of knowledge.** Hayek was certainly correct in
arguing that every individual's knowledge is incomplete. His
attempt at resolving this problem centered on a logical model
of the market. Yet the knowledge produced by markets is
rather one dimensional, consisting primarily of determining
prices or, in the case of competitions, some substitute for price.
Another and often better approach to knowledge creation is
through scholarly communities and invisible colleges (Crane
1972). Such communities have long served higher education
and research. Although they cannot ever guarantee certainty,
and can sometimes lead us astray, they have allowed us to pursue our individual and collective ends with considerable success. They are essential if we are to address the crises described
above.

**Markets are forms of governance.** Neoliberals are right in arguing that markets can be actively constructed, performed. They
make their case in at least a partially reflexive manner, apply-
ing the principles of governance to governance itself. However,
they fail to recognize that there are many, perhaps an infi-
nite number of ways of constructing and performing markets.
Markets need not be performed with economic efficiency in
mind; they can be and are often performed so as to promote
energy efficiency, equity or fairness, the use or avoidance of
various substances, safety, minimizing pollution, and so on.

Each of these values will lead to different market outcomes. One implication of this is that the neoliberal assertion that the market mechanism is based on an irrefutable logical model is false; although the interior angles of plane triangles sum to 180°, triangles drawn on spheres can exceed this number. The determination of a market price reflects supply and demand but only within the context of a set of laws and rules imposed to promote certain values.

Put differently, markets are forms of governance. Although the participants may well take a given market or competition for granted, someone or some group has to establish the rules, ensure that they are consistently enforced, and establish sanctions for those who do not follow the rules. Engaging in these tasks is a *political* act. In deliberately transforming institutions into markets, while claiming that those markets follow an irrefutable logical model, neoliberals engage in a political sleight of hand. This allows them to claim simultaneously that largely public functions such as education can be turned into markets or market-like competitions by changing legal and administrative rules, even as they claim that the outcomes of these changes are simply the natural functioning of the market.

In addition, markets are only one among many justifications to which we appeal to settle nonviolent disputes. Others include inspiration (common in religion and art), renown (of considerable concern in representative democracies), the civic (essential to the functioning of governments and maintenance of infrastructure), the industrial (in designing new technologies), and the domestic (in recognizing personal obligations to others) (Boltanski and Thévenot 1991; cf. Walzer 1983). Each of these justifications and doubtless others can and should be found in universities and research institutes. These various justifications often conflict. Attempting to justify everything via the market denies the complexity and scope of human activity. One might even say that it undermines the very liberties that it claims to defend.

**Educated citizens are essential for democracy; without democracy, liberty is illusory.** Social life in a democracy demands an educated citizenry. Hence, education, whether at the elementary, secondary, or tertiary level, should be approached as a public good rather than a merely private one (see Box 1). Only an educated citizenry can maintain the institutions of democratic life. But not any form of education will do. Democracy and liberty require a broad, "liberal" education, in which students (1) learn how their selves are constructed, (2) are exposed to a wide range of political views, (3) learn how to think critically, and (4) are able to evaluate existing and proposed policies, programs, and technologies. Much the same can be said about research institutes.

In contrast, current trends inspired by neoliberalisms discourage these values. Higher education is to be focused on the return on investment—in monetary terms—in the form of a higher future income stream. From this perspective, the notion of public financing of higher education appears superfluous; after all, higher education is merely a personal investment. This also undermines the ideal of universal access to higher education as a means of generating an educated citizenry, of ensuring that democratic ideals (even if never fully recognized in practice) are widely shared and understood.

**Addressing the crises that confront us requires that we imagine, debate, and enact new futures.** Although the various crises noted above may be viewed as disconnected, largely

**Box 1**

**Private and Public Goods**

Hundreds of volumes have been written in attempts to distinguish between public and private goods. One reason is that such definitions require assumptions that may prove false, contestable, or culturally bound. Private goods are usually defined as those goods the use of which is restricted to those who own them. Hence, my car is a private good in that I control who will use the car and under what conditions. Excepting certain extraordinary conditions, it is not available to others without permission. However, private goods are private only to the extent that some governing authority maintains a social order in which a specific bundle of rights connected to a given good is enforced. That bundle of rights may vary over time and space.

In contrast, economists usually argue that public goods are both nonexcludable and nonrivalrous (cf. Mirowski 2011). Hence, air is a public good in that no one can be excluded from partaking of it, and my breathing it does not in any way prevent you from doing the same. Under certain conditions, if poorly managed, this may lead to overuse or abuse of a given good. This is the case for air. Long seen as a public good that required no management, it is now subject to governance through anti-pollution laws.

In short, whether something is a private or public good is largely a question of social norms, customs, traditions, standards, and laws. No single definition can be used *ex ante* to define private and public goods; in a democratic society, they must be defined through deliberation.

technical problems, none of them brooks simple solutions. Amelioration of one problem may exacerbate others. Moreover, as important as new technologies may be, addressing these crises also requires us to reimagine our collective future. This cannot be accomplished unless we are all participants in an ongoing dialogue about what kind of future we want to construct. In particular, we must ask how we can maintain and even expand our liberties as we address the crises. Those of us in higher education and research have a special obligation to create selves who understand what is at stake and have a sufficiently "liberal" view of the world to create that future.

***

As I illustrate below, many of the seemingly disparate changes in higher education over the last four decades can be traced to the enacting of neoliberalisms. They substitute markets and market-like competitions for both direct governmental actions and cooperative endeavors. For example, a student deciding to go to a given university might weigh the rankings of that university on one or more measures—its Shanghai rankings, salaries paid or research productivity of the faculty, the success of graduates in obtaining suitable employment—against the financial costs of attending, the distance from home, how difficult it might be to obtain a degree, as well as high school grades, scores on standardized tests, and other admissions criteria. According to neoliberals, this approach, which inserts education within a service provider–customer relationship, optimizes the choices (i.e., the liberties) available to the prospective student, even as it spurs universities to be more efficient in their use of funds.

Furthermore, to transform students into customers, universities and research institutes have been transformed. This has been accomplished by (1) reducing government spending, (2) furthering separation between teaching and research by making a sharp distinction between permanent and temporary faculty and valuing research far more than teaching, (3) focusing teaching on the requirements of jobs that students may obtain after graduation, (4) blurring notions of scientific authorship, (5) focusing research on commercial needs, (6) enhancing intellectual property rules such that more and more knowledge is proprietary, and (7) restrictions on the production of research as well as promoting its dissemination in commercial channels (Lave, Mirowski, and Randalls 2010).

Moreover, universities around the world have been forced to engage in activities analogous to those of the private sector. Universities have become obsessed with annual rankings, the equivalent of quarterly profits. In addition, universities have engaged in product differentiation and innovation. Hence, some universities have remodeled dormitories to make them more attractive to (and to extract higher rents from) students. Others have attracted a "star" scholar—perhaps a Nobel Prize winner or member of a national academy—who appears rarely on campus but lends an air of erudition to the university. Apparently this approach works to a considerable degree. One US study of university choice notes that concern over academic quality is confined to high-achieving students. The others appear to be attracted in large part by "consumption amenities" (Jacob, McCall, and Stange 2013).

In examining higher education and research below, I emphasize the developments in the United States and the United Kingdom because these nations took the lead in enacting neoliberalism under the Reagan and Thatcher regimes, respectively. However, I shall also show how neoliberalisms have been and continue to be performed elsewhere—in places as different as France and China.

These developments can be seen in at least four distinct but overlapping areas: (1) administration, (2) education, (3) research, and (4) public engagement. Moreover, in each of these areas over the last 30 to 40 years, we have witnessed a double transformation. Both institutions of higher education and research as well as our very selves have been (re)made to serve markets and competitions. Let us begin by examining administrative changes and their consequences.

# Administration

Although all universities and research institutes worthy of the name have some administrative staff, the scope, division of labor, activities, conventions, and expectations of those administrators vary considerably across organizations, jurisdictions, regions, and nations. Despite this great variety, over the last 30 to 40 years, a number of sometimes subtle yet obvious changes have occurred. Nearly all can be traced to the neoliberalization of public universities and research institutes. In particular, *administrators have been given greater formal autonomy as long as they play the neoliberal game of competition.* In other words, administrators now find fewer direct legal barriers to action, although these vary considerably across and even within nations. However, the removal of legal barriers is linked to new modes of market-like competition, which create a variety of new reporting requirements, rules, and barriers, thereby limiting the ability of administrators to act independently. Boer and Jongbloed (2012, 558) explain, "Performance as measured by means of the number of graduates, study progress, academic output (e.g. publications or citations) or successful valorisation (e.g. number of patents) may be translated into a financial reward (or sanction) for institutions. A desire for potential gains and a fear for possible losses are expected to drive institutions towards high quality and efficient service delivery."

This hardly implies that the State is retreating or reducing its role in higher education. To the contrary, through the establishment of various forms of competition and the focus on measurable outcomes, the State has actually tightened its grip on higher education in the name of an elusive claim to efficiency. Hence, the seemingly technical project of neoliberalism—establishing markets to improve efficiency—is actually a highly prescriptive, value-laden, and controlling project. This change in the means of governance has had numerous repercussions.

**Changing roles and increasing numbers of administrators.** Over the last several decades, we have seen both a change in the role of administrators as well as an increase in their numbers. Although informal contact with colleagues in other nations suggests that this is more or less true in most nations, I have only been able to uncover reasonably reliable data for the United States. In the United States, the number of administrators has increased as university reporting requirements of national and sometimes regional or local governments have become more and more burdensome.[1] According to one analysis of 193 research universities in the United States (Greene, Kisida, and Mills 2010, 1), "Between 1993 and 2007, the number of full-time administrators per 100 students at America's leading universities grew by 39 percent, while the number of employees engaged in teaching, research or service only grew by 18 percent. Inflation-adjusted spending on administration per student increased by 61 percent during the same period, while instructional spending per student rose 39 percent." Similarly, a study by the US Department of Education suggests that "employment of administrators jumped 60 percent from 1993 to 2009, 10 times the growth rate for tenured faculty" (Hechinger 2012).

Although there is doubtless some truth to the notion that administrators have the ability to increase their share of the pie with greater ease than faculty, staff, or students, this is likely a minor aspect of the problem. US universities now must report crimes on campus, textbooks ordered, salaries and career paths of graduates, incidents of sexual harassment, diversity procedures, extramural research grants received and administered, gender equality in sports, and services provided for persons with disabilities, among other things. Some 50 new administrative rules were implemented with respect to research grants since 1991, even as the federal government put a cap on the costs of research grant administration (Leshner and Fluharty 2012). Moreover, different agencies often have different reporting requirements (because different legislative committees and units of the executive branch put those rules in place). Ostensibly, this reporting makes it easier for "customers" to determine which university they wish to attend, as well as providing legislators and the general public with useful information about the effectiveness of university operations.

In other nations such as Britain and France, national "quality assurance" agencies have been established to monitor university performance. These agencies, often only weakly accountable to legislators, add yet another layer of bureaucratic rule making and often unaccountable auditing to the freedom to operate that universities are alleged to gain. Quite obviously, they employ a considerable number of bureaucrats and administrators.

As noted above, both university administrators and government bureaucrats (differently in different nations) have produced and responded to the competitions among universities through NPM. NPM policies "… are characterized by a combination of free market rhetoric and intensive managerial control practices" (Lorenz 2012, 600) (see Box 2). In short, in the name of enhanced accountability, efficiency, transparency, and quality, they have increased the frequency, detail, and importance of collecting massive amounts of data on the "productivity" of university faculty and the overall operation of the university. Moreover, NPM has been used to transform the reward structures and monitor the performance of faculty, students, and staff in an effort to promote market values and selected ways of measuring

---

**Box 2**

**The Unwinnable Race to the Top: Lancaster University**

For several years, I was on the faculty at Lancaster University, where I found my colleagues to be intellectually challenging and collegial. But like all English universities, administrators there are under enormous pressure to perform in ways that raise the rankings in various measures. During my stay in Lancaster, each member of the faculty received an email from the then Vice-Chancellor, Paul Wellings (2010), that included the following:

Lancaster's current set of [Times Higher Education (THE)] rankings is a testament to the efforts of staff across the university. The University was ranked 124th in the THE World Ranking which is our best result to date.

Two factors made large contributions to our success. First, the fact that the Arts and Humanities ranked 31st is a considerable achievement and, second, the University's overall high citation score demonstrates the significance and relevance of all our research.

While we all know that there will be volatility in these measures from year to year, we also know that our 1:10:100 target (Top in the North-West, Top 10 in England, Top 100 in the World) is now achievable. ….

The results of the 6th National Student Survey … show very high levels of overall satisfaction with the experience at Lancaster. However, there was a drop in satisfaction from 89% to 87%. It is important that the University plays close attention to these data and that Departments with poorer scores sort out local issues.

What Professor Wellings must surely have known, given his doctorate and numerous publications in ecology, is that the statistics he cites are fundamentally flawed. There are several issues to highlight about this email. First, the THE, since 2010 has been compiled by Thompson Reuters, the same company that produces the Web of Science.[2] Although arguably better than some other indicators, in 2010, some 32.5% of the ranking score was based on the highly biased citation indicators produced by that company. Moreover, 30% of the score was based on research volume, income, and reputation (Times Higher Education Supplement 2010). Whether this was controlled for the differing sizes of universities is unclear. Indeed, full disclosure would mean that anyone with access to the proper information could reproduce the results, thereby undermining *The Times*'s monopoly on those results. But this in turn means that, unlike all good science, *the results of these ranking cannot be replicated*.

Furthermore, it is entirely unclear what being "at the top" means, given the wide range of activities of universities. For example, the term "satisfaction" is vague. It could mean that students received a first-rate education, but it could also easily mean that they found the programs easy to complete and the faculty were friendly and gave high grades. Moreover, it assumes (wrongly) that students are customers—consumers of the products offered at the university. Finally, even if a 2% drop is statistically significant, it is clearly not substantively so. Being concerned about it is at least as problematic as noting an increase in the THE ranking of the university.

them—without subjecting them to any serious debate. Indeed, much as in former communist states, NPM puts control firmly in the hands of largely unaccountable bureaucrats.[3] Ironically, "... the illusory solution to the fiscal crisis in higher education is to monitor, regulate, and reduce the costs of intellectual production, but to do so requires an ever larger, and more coercive, administrative apparatus" (Barrow 2010, 321).

As a result, faculty and staff must devote a growing percentage of their time to ever more elaborate administrative tasks such as annual merit, tenure and promotion, and departmental reviews, as well as a seemingly endless barrage of forms to be filled out about virtually every aspect of one's work. Such forms cannot merely be dismissed; they encourage those who are audited to think about and enact their work in certain ways, to note how their activities conform (or not) to certain norms implicit in the forms (Rose and Miller 1992) (see Box 3). All of this is in addition to the administrative burden associated with research grants as discussed below.

Furthermore, neoliberals have rarely if ever included the work of collecting, analyzing, and acting on those data as a real cost (e.g., Barrow 2010). Government bureaucrats (mandated by legislators to collect and act on certain kinds of information) use that information to rank universities in various ways, including the "efficiency" of their use of State funds, the graduation rates of their students, the time required to complete a degree, the salaries of recent graduates, the economic value of competitive grants received, and so on.

These rankings,[4] however poorly designed, have real consequences for the universities involved. For example, consider that there are, broadly conceived, three ways to increase graduation rates: One can provide extra support for students who are having

**Box 3**
**A Form of Governance**
Recently, my university undertook a study as part of an "initiative to enhance the diversity and quality of MSU faculty and their work environment, ..." Each faculty member was requested to complete an online survey.

In almost every instance, the questions on the survey assumed widespread agreement on the current situation where little or no evidence existed of such agreement. Consider the following: The survey posed a series of statements about promotion and tenure, to which respondents were to specify a level of agreement such as, "I have a clear understanding of the promotion/tenure process in my unit" (Woodruff 2013, 3). However, the statements failed to address whether the respondents thought the existing criteria and processes for tenure and promotion *were the right ones*.

Similarly, the questions about tensions between family obligations and workload masked the obvious. Untenured faculty are under increasing pressure to compete in an unwinnable race among individual faculty, departments, and universities based on flawed rankings that would never pass muster in an elementary statistics class. Moreover, that pressure has increased annually over the 27 years I have worked at MSU. Younger faculty members are obsessed with meeting ever-rising expectations for the production of journal articles, to the detriment of teaching, advising graduate students, university service, and even coming into the office to work and converse with colleagues. Ultimately, this encourages faculty to do mundane research and divide their work into ever smaller pieces, rather than produce a few excellent papers. Yet none of these issues was even hinted at in the survey.

Furthermore, a series of questions were asked about "MSU's culture of high performance." Like most faculty, I had no idea what that might mean.[5] Of course, without knowing what it means, the answers are essentially meaningless as well. However, that in no way stopped the designers of the survey from including statements such as, "In your view, to what extent are the following attributes representative of the culture [of high performance] in your unit?" (Woodruff 2013, 16). This was followed by a series of boxes to check (from strongly agree to strongly disagree) as to whether the unit goals were articulated and measurable, and whether high standards had been set. However, it failed to ask the preliminary questions about the proverbial elephant in the room: Are the standards the right ones? Are the measures appropriate? Are they measuring what they claim to measure? Without answers to these questions, the survey merely reproduces a gloss on the neoliberal policies adopted and fails to address key issues about workplace organization.

The survey also suggests a more serious problem subject to several differing interpretations. It may be that the neoliberal understandings of what universities are all about are so widespread among administrators that they are unaware of these concerns. Alternatively, it may be that administrators are afraid to raise these questions because they see them as a potential challenge to their authority. Either way, the survey encourages faculty to consider certain aspects of their work environment as fixed and agreed on. Whether that is in fact the case is an empirical question.

difficulties, including special tutoring and remedial courses. Alternatively, one can encourage grade inflation, thereby moving students who would otherwise fail through the university. Finally, one can restrict admissions to those who will be most likely to graduate. Of course, because funds are always in short supply, the first method is usually ruled out; the other two are at least tacitly encouraged.

Moreover, the information collected is used by administrators to grant or deny tenure and promotion, pursue or reject merit increases, make what are usually called market adjustments in salaries of individual faculty, and market their respective universities through advertising of various sorts. In short, NPM has allowed (or perhaps required) administrators to put into place market-like mechanisms and promote market values in places where the legitimacy of such values should be at best questionable.

**Shift from academics to managers as administrators.** We can also see a subtle but important shift in the notion of what it means to be an administrator. In the past, administrators tended to be academics or researchers who temporarily took on administrative roles; more recently, universities and research institutes have begun to hire administrators who have managerial rather than academic backgrounds. Although such persons may arguably be able to improve the efficiency of universities, it is far less clear that they are able to improve their quality.

**Creation of administrative careers.** Related to the shift to full-time managers and the higher salaries of administrators is the creation of administrative careers. It is now no longer uncommon for administrators to spend most of their careers in administrative posts. They are rarely if ever to be found in the classroom, laboratory, or library. Such persons often move from institution to institution as a means of climbing the increasingly corporate university or research institute ladder. Moreover, given that they are often disconnected from those who teach and/or engage in research, their views and actions with respect to universities and research organizations tend to differ markedly from those directly engaged in those activities.

**Growth in salaries of top administrators.** It will come as no surprise that salaries of top administrators of universities and (to a lesser extent) research institutes have grown far more rapidly than have those of faculty and staff. Total compensation for US public university presidents can now run as high as ~\$2 million per year (The Chronicle of Higher Education 2013), the median being \$248,000 per year. In contrast, the median salary for a full professor at a doctorate-granting university has remained level at about \$87,000 per year (The Chronicle of Higher Education 2011). This parallels the growing gap in salaries between top management and ordinary workers found throughout the corporate world. It is generally justified on the grounds that very high salaries are necessary to attract the best talent to these high-level positions. Yet, curiously, this appeared unnecessary just a few decades ago. It is particularly disturbing coming as it does in the midst of declining public support for higher education and research.[6]

**Growth in advertising and marketing of universities and research institutes.** As few as 50 years ago, universities and research institutes rarely advertised their offerings. Information about universities was available through catalogs and various compendia available in bookstores and public libraries. Information about research institutes was perhaps available in short brochures available to visitors. Today, both tend to have large and growing marketing offices. Currently confined to the rich nations, middle-income nations are beginning to do the same. For example, one of the central messages of a recent report to the Malaysian government was "… the need for local higher education institutions to engage in self-promoting activities in the outside world" (Mok 2011, 3). These offices attempt to "sell" the organization to prospective students, faculty, legislators, research funding agencies, private corporations, and donors. Such marketing efforts often emphasize the scores obtained on a wide range of rankings. In some instances, institutions even pay to be included in these rankings. At best it is questionable whether such rankings serve their intended purposes. In addition, with respect to US universities, in a recent poll of admissions directors, only 14% felt the rankings were useful to students in choosing among institutions (Houry 2013).

Moreover, even if they do serve their intended purposes, they also promote precisely the kind of unethical behavior that universities and research institutes are supposed to avoid. Hence, in their efforts to promote their institutions in academic rankings, administrators at three well-known and respected US universities—George Washington University, Claremont-McKenna College, and Emory University—deliberately inflated their scores.

Furthermore, universities market themselves not only to the "outside world" but to those who are part of the university community. My university recently revamped its internal webpage with news about the university. Moreover, recently every member of the faculty and staff received an effusive email telling us about the new look for one of several weekly electronic newsletters. Glossy brochures proliferate telling anyone willing to read them about the herculean feats performed in research, academics, sports, environmental protection, traffic flow, and so on.

Finally, it is worth noting that funds used for internal and external marketing are not otherwise available for research or education. Given the scope and growth of the marketing apparatus, this is hardly a trivial sum.

**Growth in numbers of part-time and temporary (adjunct) faculty.** The flip side of the growth in administration is the growth in the number of adjunct faculty and short-term research appointments. These people—who now constitute about 75% of the faculty at US universities—are hired on fixed term appointments and have little or no opportunity to become permanent members of the faculty. They are usually poorly paid and overworked, yet they make up a large and growing portion of the faculty. Over the last several decades, they have created a two-class system for faculty appointments: those who are hired in part-time and temporary positions and those who are full-time permanent employees.

**Changing sources of university and research institute financial support.** The decline in State support to universities and research institutes has led both administrators and those in State agencies to consider other major sources of support: tuition, public and private sector competitive grants, and donations. Tuition has been raised substantially in many nations over the last several decades, but its growth has been slowed by objections from some legislators who argue (occasionally with some justification) that universities are inefficient and engage in outdated practices.

In the United States, competition for and receipt of public sector research grants has been encouraged by the awarding of "startup costs" to new faculty members. Initially found only in the natural sciences and engineering, where labs are necessary accoutrements for most research, startup costs are now commonly made available to social sciences and humanities faculty as well. Some years ago, receipt of grant funds was seen solely as an extra. Now it is often seen as a central criterion for awarding merit increases and promotions.

Corporate research grants have also been encouraged in a variety of ways. First, the older barriers to collaboration between universities and public research institutes and the private sector have been reduced or eliminated. Yet such relations might be rejected for many reasons that remain largely unaddressed: conflicts of interest, public subsidies to one firm to the detriment of others, and the private sector's desire to keep knowledge protected versus the public sector's desire to make knowledge public. Despite these issues, public–private collaborations of all kinds are very much in vogue. Second, these are supplemented by the formation of university-led industrial research parks, and in some cases by the building of new facilities that permit university and industry scientists to work side by side. A $500 million investment by BP at the University of California Berkeley is a case in point; it has been the subject of continuing conflict between administrators and some faculty.

Finally, many universities and research institutes have expanded their development offices, seeking donations from wealthy alumni, large corporations, and large foundations. Special facilities have been built in which to entertain donors and a variety of arrangements have been made with those willing and able to donate large sums. Occasionally, this approach backfires, as donors demand to take an active involvement in university or research institute affairs. This is true of both foundations that now engage in "strategic philanthropy" and wealthy individuals and corporations that feel obligated to ensure that their funds are used in certain ways. The former often saddle grant recipients with the need for measurable goals and outcomes, such that larger, more creative, and longer term projects become impossible. The latter often attempt to directly intervene in university affairs, leading to clashes with administrators and, in some cases, withdrawal of funds (Katz 2012).

**Universities by the numbers.** The entire shift toward markets and competitions has pushed administrators to govern universities as much as possible by numbers. Indeed, a European study noted that "... at least 980 universities proposed, in their mission statements, to achieve a high level of international excellence in research [as measured by scores in various rankings]. It reflects both an unrealizable aspiration and a lost potential for many other areas where universities bring benefit to their communities" (Boulton 2010, 6). Yet numbers, usually in the form of quantitative data collected from convenience samples, appear to have a kind of concreteness, although nothing is quite as abstract as numbers.

Consider the "discovery" in 2003 that French universities lagged behind those of other countries in the Shanghai rankings. This sparked a great deal of concern and considerable reorganization of French higher education and research along largely neoliberal lines. That said, it appears few politicians or academics spent much time examining the formulation of those rankings. As it turns out, the Shanghai rankings, developed at Shanghai Jiao Tong University, are at best a poor (or extremely limited) measure of quality. As Gingras (2008, 8–9) explains:

It is composed of six measures of which four have a weight of 20% each: 1) the members of the faculty who have received a Nobel prize or a Fields Medal (for mathematicians), 2) the number of researchers at the institution who are on the "most cited" list of Thomson Reuters, 3) the number of articles from the institution published in *Nature* or *Science*, 4) the total number of articles listed in the Web of Science by the Thomson Reuters company. Two other measures each have a weight of 10%: 5) the number of former students who have received a Nobel Prize or a Fields Medal, 6) an adjustment of the preceding results according to the size of the institution. It is clearly evident that the final index of success is based on several heterogeneous measures, because the number of publications in *Science* and *Nature* is not commensurable with the number of Nobel Prizes. Even more surprising, it has been shown that the data on which it is founded are difficult to reproduce.

In addition, the focus of the rankings is entirely on the natural sciences and engineering. No attempt is made to include the social sciences, arts, or humanities. Nor does the measure include anything about teaching and learning. The use of the Web of Science gives the entire exercise an Anglo-American bias. In short, what we have is a highly flawed measure that was accepted at face value.[7]

Nevertheless, the French government engaged in reorganization at considerable cost. Universities were linked more closely to the *Grandes Ecoles* and research institutes through the creation of "Poles of research and higher education." Attempts made to restrict university admissions provoked considerable pushback from both high school and university students. The passage of a law somewhat misnamed the "Liberties and Responsibilities of Universities" (LRU) forced universities to compete for the meager funds allotted to them. World Class Universities Programmes (WCUPs) were created by mergers among institutions and reorganization promoting various kinds of competition. Several large national bureaucracies, including France's Evaluation Agency for Research and Higher Education (AERES), were created (Cremonini et al. 2013). Not surprisingly, virtually no change occurred in France's position in the Shanghai rankings.

That said, reforms such as those in France and elsewhere have pressed nearly every large research university and institute to establish some sort of office that collects and analyzes massive amounts of numerical data about the institution in order to engage in what have become global competitions. Similarly, State agencies that monitor higher education and research also maintain such databases. One tendency (also common in the business world) is to attempt to govern both universities and research institutes largely by these numerical data.

However, the search for the perfect metric is at best illusory
for several reasons. First, many of the things for which universities are designed are difficult or impossible to put in numerical
terms. For example, it is easy to measure the percentage of
students who graduate within five years but much more difficult to measure what they have learned. It is easy to count the
number of publications produced by a faculty member but far
more difficult to measure their import. It is easy to count the
number of persons attending public meetings organized by university or research institute faculty but far more difficult to
determine whether they found the information exchanged at
those meetings sufficiently valuable to be taken seriously and
acted on.

For many metrics that involve human activity, those measured will restructure their behavior so as to maximize their
scores. In contrast, when measuring the growth rate of a bacte-
rial culture, the measure used has little or no effect on the bacteria. This means that almost as soon as a new human metric is put
into place, those measured adjust their behavior in ways that (at
least potentially) undermine the very metric employed. It is perhaps best expressed as Campbell's (1979, 85, emphasis in original) Law: *"The more any quantitative social indicator is used for
social decision-making, the more subject it will be to corruption pressures and the more apt it will be to distort and corrupt the social processes it is intended to monitor."*

Furthermore, metrics may give those in charge the impression that the metric eliminates the need for judgment. In point
of fact, however, metrics never substitute for judgment. One
must always determine whether a given bit of information con-
forms to the categories defined in the metric. As statistician
Marcello Boldrini (1972, 203) noted some years ago, "[t]he truth

is that without starting from the formation of cases, there can be no induction: here begins the creation of the uniformity of nature by the human mind, from which are produced the structures of every factual regularity." Moreover, often those who are charged with analyzing the data generated by the metrics in question have little or no direct connection with the data-collection process. Hence, they may well make erroneous assumptions about just what the data mean. For example, they may assume that the subject students spend the most time on is the one they are most interested in pursuing, but that might not be the case at all (Parry 2012).

Moreover, as contrasted with data for scientific and scholarly research, data from forms, webpages, directories, test scores, and other materials designed for other purposes may contain many errors. Hence, for example, it is well established that citation counts from Google Scholar, Scopus, and the Web of Science give different results. None of these databases was designed with the creation of faculty productivity metrics in mind.

Finally, virtually none of the numbers includes measures of student experience and learning, diversity of the student body, democratization of higher education, or the independence of thought and action—*the liberty*—of scholars. Instead, most are focused on making universities and research institutes even more elitist in their organization by (1) increasing competition among students to be admitted, (2) increasing concern among administrators (and perhaps faculty) about enhancing the relative rankings of the institution in question, (3) using indicators to focus the attention of scholars on those things that are easily measured and deemed politically desirable by elites, and (4) discouraging interaction between scholars and those outside the scholarly world.

In summary, as a result of a wide range of legislative and executive policies implemented by various governments over the last three to four decades, the administration of universities and research institutes has been restructured so as to undermine collegiality and promote managerial control and hierarchy. This has been done (allegedly) in the name of efficiency in the use of public funds. But it has promoted vast bureaucracies at each institution and in government agencies that are both opaque and largely unaccountable. As we shall see, it has transformed higher education and research in ways that treat scholars and students as isolates, reduce their autonomy and freedoms, and undermine free inquiry.

# Education

**From public good to private good.** Higher education has shifted from a public good provided by the State to a private good provided based on consumer demand (see Box 4). Hence, higher education is no longer regulated by direct State intervention but from a distance, through the market. Student choice is made central; responding to students' preferences is a requirement for a successful university. This is one reason that private for-profit organizations like the US-based University of Phoenix were created. They are able to capitalize (literally!) on the notion that higher education is solely an investment in one's self, an investment designed to enhance future earnings. Put differently, higher education is viewed as little different from investing in the stock market or a business. Indeed, investment banker Merrill Lynch, in a report titled *The Book of Knowledge*, estimated that the "education and training industry" alone is now worth $2 trillion (Moe, Bailey, and Lau 1999).

Clearly, when tuition rates in public institutions are low, the private sector has little or no opportunity to compete. Hence, private for-profit tertiary education used to be limited to specialized technical training. However, as tuition has risen, private for-profit universities have flourished. They tend to

Box 4

**The Case of Newcastle University**

Newcastle University, with its main campus in England, provides an excellent example of the institutional transformation underway. A glossy brochure promoting the university is titled "The Idea of a World-Class Civic University." In it, Vice-Chancellor Chris Brink briefly discusses Cardinal Newman's argument for a broad-based liberal arts education (from which the brochure's title borrows) and von Humboldt's emphasis on research driven by curiosity. However, it then redefines the notion of a public good: "However, we believe that our role in the knowledge economy is not only to create knowledge and educate students. Universities are not there simply to confer a private benefit; they should also serve as a public good. For us the question is not only 'What are we good at?,' but also 'What are we good for?'" (Newcastle University 2013, 3). He then provides a response. The response is defined in terms of publications, citations, and "reputation and esteem indicators," as well as (re)defining the university in terms of the supply and demand for knowledge.

It is important to recognize in this statement what would have been an anathema 40 or 50 years ago. First, providing students with an education and engaging in research along the lines described by Newman and Humboldt, respectively, are now viewed as private goods. The idea that society as a whole might benefit from these actions is dismissed; these goods are implicitly regarded as the result of a sound investment of and in human capital. Second, the quality of research is defined in terms of easily measured New Public Management indicators. Third, the civic mission is actually reduced by redefining it in terms of well-defined problems facing society. The question "What are we good at?" suggests that the university is merely one among many transposable tools available to society to advance predetermined societal goals. The notion that curiosity-driven research of the sort advocated by von Humboldt might lead to public or civic goods by identifying otherwise unrecognized problems or redefining the way in which we understand our world is at least implicitly dismissed. Instead, most of the research projects currently underway that are noted in the brochure address issues of immediate public concern: computer-assisted learning, personalized medicine, the use of bacteria in medical treatments and improvement drug development, among others.

None of this is to suggest that the research cited in the brochure is of poor quality or unbefitting of a university. However, it does suggest that, even at a major British university, the emphasis has shifted toward the neoliberal approach to education and research.

offer education on the cheap, with part-time faculty and minimal or no campuses, laboratories, or library facilities. Although some of them have done well financially, many have poor records of student placement. Others have violated various laws with respect to loans (Blumenstyk 2011) and recruiters' claims (Mytelka 2010). Their students also had lower pass rates on licensing exams than those from nonprofit schools as well as higher student loan debts for bachelor's degrees (Government Accountability Office 2011). Similar for-profit institutions have opened in Britain and continental Europe, although as of yet on a smaller scale.

However, the restructuring of English universities has promoted for-profit universities: It enhances the market for such private education, which will undoubtedly now be much less expensive than that offered by English universities. Among the likely beneficiaries is BPP University College. Like the University of Phoenix, it is part of the Apollo Group, a US company with a heavy investment from the Carlisle Group, a private equity firm (Finlayson 2010).

**Shift from public support for higher education to individual support.** As a result of the shift to a "user pays" model, students in many nations are now increasingly saddled with extraordinarily high loan payments when they graduate. In the United States, rising tuition (the result of declining state appropriations) has put students into considerable debt. The approximately $1 trillion in total student debt now exceeds consumer debt (*Washington Times* 2012). This has several effects. First, it means that students are pressured to choose their majors to a great extent based on expectations of future earnings; after all, they will need to pay back these loans during the most productive years of their careers.[1] One US national study found that more than half of seniors chose their field of study based on their "ability to find a job" (National Survey of Student Engagement 2012).

Second, many students are now forced to work as many as 30 to 40 hours per week while attending the university to limit the size of their loans. This includes not only conventional jobs but also selling blood plasma, performing erotic acts on the web, selling eggs and sperm at fertilization clinics, and paid participation in drug trials (Troop 2013). As a result, they have less time for intellectual work.

Third, because universities have been forced to raise tuition as State funding has declined, the proportion of total costs borne by students continues to rise. This is particularly true in the United States, but it is also the case in many other nations. Furthermore, there is at least some evidence that the heavy financial burden has a direct effect on educational performance for about one-third of undergraduates (Sander 2012). In addition, students report refraining from the purchase of required materials due to the costs of education (National Survey of Student Engagement 2012). Ironically, students report a shift away from entrepreneurial activities on graduation as a result of the large loans that must be repaid (Louis 2013). In summary, shifting the burden of higher education from public tax-based support to individual support often financed by student loans has been a costly failure for both the students involved as well as nations as a whole.

Recently, England changed its way of financing higher education such that it looks much like that in the United States. As the Browne Report (Browne 2010) noted,

> What we recommend is a radical departure from the existing way in which HEIs [Higher Education Institutions] are financed. Rather than the Government providing a block grant for teaching to HEIs, their finance now follows the student who has chosen and been admitted to study. Choice is in the hands of the student. HEIs can charge different and higher fees provided that they can show improvements in the student experience and demonstrate progress in providing fair access and, of course, students are prepared to entertain such charges.

In short, the entire system has been reorganized so as to allow the State to operate at a distance. The report is replete with emphasis on "value for money," "student choice," "greater autonomy for institutions," and so on. In point of fact, however, education has been redefined as an economic investment for each student. In keeping with the neoliberal perspective pioneered by Gary Becker, students are to be treated as investors of human capital seeking a monetary return in the form of higher salaries. The more debt they incur, the more obsessed with the monetary rewards of a university degree they will be.

At the same time, the report is silent on the notion that education should prepare students for citizenship in a democratic society, allow them to appreciate the arts and humanities, or provide them with critical thinking skills. Moreover, the Science,

Technology, Engineering, and Mathematics (STEM) disciplines are to be subsidized even as support is eliminated for the humanities and social sciences, thus violating the market-based notion on which it is claimed that the new system is based. The alleged freedom of choice for students now glosses over the substantial differences in costs across disciplines. Moreover, individual student loans not yet paid are only erased 30 years after graduation. In short, many students will have passed much of their lives in substantial indebtedness.

Furthermore, the Browne Report (Browne 2010) notes that "[w]e recognise that public investment in higher education is reducing." Yet it fails to ask the obvious question: Why is this the case? Instead, through the use of the passive voice, a reduction in State support for higher education is described as a natural phenomenon. Indeed, the idea that higher education is a public good is abandoned; it is to be practiced instead as another investment subject to the discipline of the marketplace.

Finally, the entire project is based on the fallacious argument that students can make a meaningful choice when provided with more information about universities (apparently in the form of salaries of graduates in various fields). Students often do not know what kind of education they *want* and are even less likely to know what kind of education they *require*. Were they to know this, they would not be in need of that education. Moreover, student choice depends in part on the ability to live in a different city; some students may lack that ability for a wide variety of reasons. In addition, predictions about the state of the job market are usually only valid for a few years; hence, the well-paid job now may be the poorly paid one at some point in the near future. Furthermore, student choice may force some institutions to close and still more to reduce the number of subjects taught as a result of declining demand, thereby reducing student choice. Finally, only in textbooks are markets perfect; the report suggests this by noting that subsidies may be required to ensure that there are sufficient entrants (to meet the needs as defined by government bureaucrats) into certain professions.

**Massive Open Online Courses (MOOCs).** The development of MOOCs has been heralded in the United States by a wide range of university administrators as well as state and national legislators. MOOCs, it would appear, are the answer to rising tuition: One finds the best teachers in the world and allows them to teach tens of thousands of students all at once. But all of this fails to recognize that so doing will create (or perhaps re-create) a two-class system for university education; those who can afford it will continue to attend real universities and pay high tuition. They will get the advantages of direct interaction with faculty, access to library facilities and laboratories, and interaction with other students. In contrast, those who cannot afford it will use MOOCs.

Even more problematic is that those at the bottom of the income ladder are usually the least prepared for MOOCs. They often lack the study skills and background knowledge needed to succeed with college-level work (Carlson and Blumenstyk 2012). Indeed, although vast numbers of students have registered for MOOCs, there is at least some evidence that they tend not to be interested in pursuing degrees, but rather in learning specific skills, and that the vast majority of them drop out before the course has ended. In short, although there may well be a role for MOOCs in higher education, that role is likely quite limited.

Of course, none of this is to suggest that information technologies cannot be successfully used by universities that have classrooms and face-to-face interaction among teachers and students. As I note below, such technologies give universities an opportunity to end the rather ineffective lecture system.

**A decline in foreign language instruction.** Just as global communications are growing in scope and declining in cost, US universities have reduced foreign language requirements and, in some cases, gutted foreign language departments. Ostensibly, this is justified by the widespread use of English as the *lingua franca* for the world of commerce and low enrollments in (the no longer required) foreign language courses. Hence, foreign language courses are seen as having high costs and few benefits. However, as a consequence of this, US students are (1) less likely to understand foreign cultures, (2) more likely to be seen as arrogant and/ or ignorant interlopers, and (3) less likely to appreciate how language shapes our world.[2]

In much of the non-English-speaking world, one finds a somewhat different situation. English-language courses tend to be exceedingly popular, in large part due to the global adoption of English as the language of commerce and increasingly of science. At the same time, instruction in other languages is now seen as far less important. This is not only problematic for small linguistic communities such as speakers of Finnish or Slovene, where there have always been few non-native students, but also for far larger language communities such as the Francophone world. As Michael Edwards, an Englishman recently elected to the *Académie Française* notes, "French philosophers and scientists are increasingly writing in English in order to be published worldwide. But if they write in English, they will cease to think in the characteristic way the French think. A whole treasure of the mind will be lost" (quoted in Metcalf 2013).

Moreover, given the dominance of English in some institutions in non-English-speaking nations, it has become the language of university instruction. Hence, INSEAD, France's premier business school, conducts nearly all of its instruction in English; its website is also entirely in English. As the website states, "To be admitted to the MBA Programme, a candidate must be fluent in English. English certification must be sent with your application" (INSEAD 2013).[3] Similarly, Wageningen University (The Netherlands) conducts all courses as well as all administrative matters in English. Much the same is true of the top universities in the Arab world (Hanafi 2011). Also nearly all Indian universities provide instruction largely in English.

The consequences of this are somewhat paradoxical. At the moment in history when the world has become so much smaller as a result of global trade, nearly instant Internet and telephone connections, and rapid, relatively inexpensive air travel, it would appear that overcoming cultural differences by learning other languages would be a high priority. Instead, we find that language instruction is becoming more limited and the cultural diversity embedded in language being squandered. Furthermore, because the elite institutions in non-English-speaking nations are much more likely than others to use English as the language of instruction, they extend the already wide gap between elites and the general population.

**Education solely as a means of maximizing one's salary.** Of late, some have taken the market approach to its obvious conclusion, estimating the "monetary value added" by obtaining a degree in a given field of study. For example, the state of Tennessee has started to produce average first-year salaries by subject for each program at each state university (Berrett 2012). Since then, they have been joined by several other states, posting the data on CollegeMeasures.org. Even on its own terms, the project has significant weaknesses. Among other things, it only includes those graduates who remain in the state. In addition, it assumes that first-year salaries are a good estimate of future earnings. Even the president of College Measures admits that "the data he's publishing is best viewed with a critical eye" (Dwoskin 2012).

In a slightly different vein, Texas A&M University has begun to calculate the monetary value added by each professor. Specifically, the university now weighs salaries "against students taught, tuition generated, and research grants obtained" (Simon and Banchero 2010). Not surprisingly, those in the humanities generally tend to provide the least value added, even sometimes producing negative values. Some legislators have suggested that such subjects would be best removed from the curriculum so as to focus more on education that would enhance one's future salary.

**Growth in testing and standardizing of knowledge.** As State financial support for teaching (including teaching assistants) has declined and pressure to apply for extramural grants has increased due to budgetary pressures, the use of standardized (and usually multiple-choice) tests has increased. This is especially true for entry-level courses, where class size can reach or exceed 1,500 students. Hence, it is all too common to find upper division and even doctoral students who cannot write a grammatically correct sentence, argue for or against a particular position, critically analyze various perspectives, or form an argument for their own view.

Moreover, as has already been the case for elementary and secondary education in many nations, pressure is building to use similar standardized tests at universities for both national and international comparisons. The claim is that standardized tests would give future students more information, enabling them to decide which university to attend, as well as providing a means to evaluate the quality of university education nationally as well as at particular institutions. All of this assumes, of course, that there is a "level playing field" from which students take these tests; yet national, cultural, regional, class, income, and other differences play a major role in test-taking success (Christou 2010).

Even were we to exclude that concern, most standardized tests tend to measure one's knowledge of "the facts" at a particular point in time and space. Moreover, many of "the facts" change over time; one need merely pick up a 10-year-old textbook to see how much that is the case. In addition, standardized tests poorly measure critical thinking, creativity, and nonmathematical problem solving—precisely the skills and abilities essential to grapple with complex problems in a rapidly changing world.

Yet even if such tests were adequate measures of student achievement, they would have the effect of overly standardizing higher education and focusing it on certain subjects and not others. In addition, it is unclear what pedagogical purposes are served by such tests. Their impact on learning has been well documented; they transform education into a "teach to the test" exercise (Apple 2006). As such, they sharply reduce creativity for faculty and students and leave little room for new knowledge. As Henry Giroux (2013) puts it, "[t]he 'disimagination machine' … functions primarily to undermine the ability of individuals to think critically, imagine the unimaginable, and engage in thoughtful and critical dialogue: put simply, to become critically informed citizens of the world."

Recently, EdX, a nonprofit firm founded by Harvard University and the Massachusetts Institute of Technology, developed automated software that it claims can grade essays. It is available for free to any institution that wishes to use it. EdX's president argues that it is an excellent pedagogical tool, as it would allow students to write essays repeatedly until they get them right. The software requires that human teachers grade the first 100 essays; it then uses artificial intelligence to take on the grading process. Assuming that it works as claimed, this software poses three related problems. First, it demands a curriculum that is highly standardized, such that hundreds of students answer the same questions. Second, it is tailor-made for those who wish yet another means to audit the performance of faculty. Third, it precludes creativity, for both faculty who might wish to teach in a creative manner as well as students who might wish to answer the questions in novel ways (Markoff 2013).

The situation in England is similar, although the organization of higher education there allows greater control by the central government. Although the new approach described in the Browne Report claims to reduce bureaucracy, in point of fact it establishes a new bureaucracy, the Higher Education Council (HEC).[4] The HEC is an independent entity that invests in "high-priority courses," ensures equity of access, sets quality standards, promotes competition for students, and resolves disputes between students and universities. In short, the HEC has the power to manipulate the newly created markets for higher education from behind the scenes to produce marketable skills based on labor market forecasts and create what its officials—rather than scholars or students—consider a "quality education."

Indeed, the United Kingdom has been active in the promotion—through educational standards, exhortations, and funding—of "enterprising education," a new form of partnership between business and government. Although linking work to education is hardly a new approach, the new partnerships go much further: "Thus the state is able to work at promoting, glorifying and embedding the values ... of 'flexibility', 'self transformation', 'competitiveness' and 'market responsibility' closely associated with neoliberalism through placing enterprise at the heart of the curriculum in both practical content and overarching ethos" (Mccafferty 2010, 542–543).

**Plagiarism.** Cheating and plagiarism have surely occurred as long as teachers have required students to complete assignments of one sort or another. However, the shift in university education from citizenship and culture to preparation for a well-paid job has brought with it enormous pressure on students to plagiarize. This has been compounded by the need for many students to work long hours while attending the university. Moreover, the rise of the Internet, although not directly connected to neoliberal policies, has made plagiarism easier by bringing into existence many businesses that thrive on it. One example should suffice to make the point, although there are many similar "services" on the web. "Lashzone" provides original papers, lab reports, and other class assignments. As they note on their website, "We offer professional assistance on post-secondary homework, assignments, essays, lab reports, assignment revision ... etc. You get the idea? We already got the degrees you are trying to get and will proudly assist you in getting one too. ... Whether it is mathematics, chemistry, literature, programming or philosophy, we have got a person for it" (Lashzone 2013).

They also attempt to relate to students in their advertising by noting that students are under considerable pressure as a result of both educational and work requirements. Students can purchase assignments from Lashzone that are written specifically for them. Hence, they do not involve directly plagiarizing from someone else's work, usually by copying parts of papers that appear on the web. Instead, they involve hiring ghost authors who write the paper based on the student's initial assignment.[5] They do this for a fee, thereby once again separating those who can pay from those who can't.

Moreover, ghost authoring is now a global business—and a highly profitable one at that. Dozens, perhaps hundreds, of websites now exist with names like Assignment Expert, AssignmentsWeb, eHomework, and AssignmentHelpWorld that are easily accessible to students and directly encourage plagiarism. Because these businesses are entirely unregulated, the quality of the work done doubtless varies; *caveat emptor* prevails. Moreover, writers are generally poorly paid, even though the companies may charge students rather hefty fees. Because both the writers and the companies they write for are scattered around the world, legal action against them is nearly impossible (Bartlett 2009). Yet their very existence is largely due to the excessive focus on value for money in higher education.

**Dumbing down higher education.** In summary, the combined effects of (1) working long hours while going to school so as to minimize the size of student loans, (2) the shift from students as learners to students as customers, (3) the common use of student evaluations to assess teaching, (4) the reduction in the numbers of permanent faculty teaching as well as the decline in support for teaching, and (5) the low priority that teaching has in many if not most research universities have each had the effect of dumbing down higher education. After all, "...a regard for the intellectual merits of the programme is pitted against the need to dumb down standards and the appeal of the course to the requirements of the market" (Hyde, Clarke, and Drennan 2013, 45). As a result, according to one recent longitudinal study of US undergraduates, students now spend about half as much time studying as they did in the 1960s, 32% did not take a single course that required reading more than 40 pages per week, and half did not take any course that required more than 20 pages of writing over the course of the semester (Arum and Roksa 2011).

# Research

What I have noted about education is equally present in the domain of research. The "human capital" approach pioneered by Gary Becker is present here much as it is with respect to students. That is, faculty are presumed to be—and for purposes of evaluation are treated as—autonomous individuals who are interested in investing their human capital, thereby enhancing their salaries. The notions of communities of scholars and invisible colleges are jettisoned. Furthermore, to promote the human capital approach, researchers are simultaneously made subject to various forms of uncertainty and insecurity even as they are expected to be loyal to institutional goals—what Gori and Del Volgo (2009), following La Boétie, call "voluntary servitude." Of course, the details play out differently in different situations. Consider some of the changes in the research process over the last several decades.

**Counting publications.** It has become fashionable to count publications, especially articles in scholarly journals, in making decisions about promotion, tenure, and merit increases. Publication counts have several distinct advantages for administrators who are required (usually by some higher authority such as the government agencies that provide funding) to audit the performance of researchers: Journal articles can be relatively rapidly completed, peer reviewed, and published. Hence, they fit relatively well into the annual reviews of scholars and departments. They also require relatively little work on the part of administrators, especially as compared with reading and evaluating the actual publications. As a result, establishing expected numbers of publications—especially in peer-reviewed journals—has become the norm in reviews of faculty. Of course, this poses several problems as scholars attempt, with more or less success, to game the system.

Quite obviously, it is possible in many fields to divide one's research into numerous small pieces and publish each as a separate article. For example, scientists who study soil percolation rates use tanks with glass beads to simulate soil profiles. They can churn out numerous papers, each reporting a somewhat different experiment. Similarly, a social scientist who engages in survey research can write numerous papers where each examines a slightly different model of relations among the variables in the survey. Even in fields such as medieval history, where books have long been the major avenue to publication, scholars feel pressure to divide their work into small pieces and to publish it in scholarly journals (Kehm and Leiðytë 2010).

In contrast, some types of research require years of work before any publishable result can emerge. For example, developing new plant varieties can easily take a decade of research. Often there is little to report before the new variety is developed. Similarly, certain forms of ethnographic research, paleontology, natural history, and ecology require years of work before publishable results emerge. Clearly, counting journal articles implicitly devalues this sort of research. Moreover, it sends a signal to persons considering pursuing such topics that they might be better off shifting to a field in which publications are more rapidly produced.

Second, the number of scientific journals has risen dramatically; hence, there is likely a home for any paper if one searches long enough (Colquhoun 2011). Quite obviously, nations that have expanded their scholarly communities greatly over the last half century—India, Brazil, and China, among others—have also produced their own scientific journals. In addition, the advent of web-based scientific journals has opened numerous opportunities for publication. One site lists 8,750 open access journals from 121 nations (DOAJ 2013). Thousands more require subscriptions from readers and/or fees from authors. Although some are legitimate journals that engage in serious peer review before publication, others are vanity presses, publishing virtually everything submitted for a substantial fee. Given the pressure to publish, it is likely that many will survive, earning a tidy profit for their owners while contributing little to any form of scholarship. Proponents of counting would do well to follow Einstein's advice: "Everything that can be counted does not necessarily count; everything that counts cannot necessarily be counted." In short, although it is easy to count publications, it is unclear just what it is that one is counting. In an attempt to resolve this problem, citation counting has become an alternative approach.

**Counting citations.** In general, authors usually have no direct control over citations to their work. As a result, administrators tend to see citations as a better means of evaluation than merely counting articles. Citation counting has emerged as commonplace in the United States, Western Europe, and Japan. In addition, "[s]cholars from China to Italy, from Belgium to South Africa, from Australia to the Nordic countries, ... rely on such data [from the Web of Science] to discuss the success, impact, and visibility of research in specific contexts" (Paasi 2005, 772; see also Gori and Del Volgo 2009).

It is useful to review just how citation counting emerged and what its intrinsic limits are. The most widely used citation database, the Web of Science, is illustrative. It was initially developed for librarians at large US universities. It was intended to provide librarians with a convenient guide to purchasing subscriptions to journals. Through citations, librarians could gauge how frequently a journal in a given discipline was used and purchase subscriptions to those journals most widely cited. In addition, because the initial audience was US librarians and indirectly US scientists, the database had and continues to have a strong English-language bias. Indeed, English-language abstracts are required for accepting journals into the database.

Currently, the Web of Science contains information about the contents of and citations to about 10,000 journals out of the approximately 100,000 journals published worldwide. As Archambault and Larivière (2009, 638) explain, this "... likely had the effect of creating a selffulfilling [sic] prophecy. Indeed, by concentrating on the US situation and by positively biasing the sources in favour of US journals, the method placed these journals on centre stage. Had a broader linguistic and national coverage been considered, it might have revealed that these journals were not in fact more cited than others." Hence, not surprisingly, the rankings of the top 20 institutions among highly cited scientists include 18 US institutions and two from the United Kingdom (Paasi 2005).

As a result of these rather grievous faults, such as indexing a skewed sample of about 10% of all journals and not indexing much of the non-journal literature at all, the Web of Science is a poor database for measuring citations of individual institutions or scholars. But the problems only begin there. Other issues include the following.

All other things being equal, scholars working in large fields will have a greater chance of being cited than those working in small fields. In other words, even if I do path-breaking work in an area with 25 other colleagues, the maximum number of citations I can have will be limited by the number of people working in that area. In contrast, if there are 5,000 people working in that area, the maximum number of citations I could potentially have would be much higher. Given that new and interdisciplinary areas are likely to be small, this implies a clear bias against innovation in research.

In addition, authors may be cited for reasons other than the validity or importance of their findings (Kumar 2010). For example, one may be cited for erroneous or even fraudulent findings. A 2004 paper by Korean researchers Hwang Woo Suk et al. (2004) has been cited 388 times,[1] largely for fraudulently claiming to have made discoveries about stem cells.

Moreover, those who cite articles rarely do so *solely* because of the quality of the paper; instead, they focus on how the article fits *rhetorically* within their own papers. Although neophytes may believe that scholarly (and especially scientific) publication merely involves engaging in careful research and publishing the results, the actual process is far more complex. As Karin Knorr Cetina (1981, 42) noted some years ago, "Scientific papers are not designed to promote an understanding of alternatives, but to foster the impression that what has been done is all that could be done." Hence, one is always constrained to write in a manner that shows that one's work helps to explain or clarify a problem defined by others in the field. Therefore, one must necessarily situate one's work within a body of literature, showing that it addresses an important issue in that field. Papers that may once have been seen as brilliant breakthroughs are not cited if their results are now considered to be common knowledge. Other papers are cited because they bolster the argument being made by the author. Still others are cited because the author's findings contradict, expand on, use similar (or different) instruments from those of the citing paper, or perhaps differ in subtle ways from the findings in the cited paper. Yet others are cited because the cited author is widely reputed in the field, but it is at the least arguable whether that person's reputation is the result of being widely cited or that person is widely cited because of her reputation. The quality of all these cited papers is certainly a consideration, but it is only one of the many reasons that one cites another paper. Thus, some high-quality papers may be rarely cited, whereas some low-quality papers may be cited frequently (Borgman and Furner 2002).

In addition, different counts of citations give different results, depending on which journals are included in a given databases, what measures are used to compute citations, and the differing forms and frequency of citations across different fields. Importantly, there is no global registry of all scholarly publications; each database is a purposive sample of publications based on what the compiling agency defines as important.

Furthermore, to compare scholars within fields, one must first determine to which field an author belongs. As research increasingly takes place at the interface between fields and disciplines, deciding where to place an author becomes more difficult.

What's more, many journal articles are co-authored; giving credit to each author is a complex process that is not uniform across fields of science (van Noorden 2010). In some fields, the first author is the lead, whereas in others the last author has that role. In still other fields—certain branches of physics are exemplary—there may be several hundred authors listed on a single paper.

Also, the number of citations in a given article varies considerably from one field to another. To compare across fields, one needs to "normalize" the citation rates. However, this is rarely done.

Finally, in some fields, journal articles are the primary means of scholarly communication. Most of the natural sciences and engineering fit into this category. However, in other fields, especially the humanities, books are the main means of communication. In the social sciences, one tends to find a mix of both journals and books. However, most of the citation databases focus on journals, thereby implicitly devaluing books and those fields of study that rely on book publication.

Most scientometrics experts decry the naïve usage of citation data to evaluate individual scholars (e.g., Braun 2010). One sums up the issue of using citations to rank scientists quite well: "There is a better way to evaluate the importance of a paper or the research output of an individual scholar: read it" (Bergstrom 2010, 870).

**Checking prestige of journals.** In addition to counting articles and citations, some administrators have begun to use the rankings of the various journals in a given field as a means of evaluating researchers. This is often accomplished by using the Journal Impact Factor (JIF) developed by the Web of Science. Similar approaches are used to evaluate book publishers. Of course, as noted above, this measure was not developed for evaluation of individual faculty members (*Nature* 2010) or even individual journals. Despite that, use of this approach means that an article appearing in *Science* would receive a higher ranking than one published in a less prestigious journal. Similarly, publishing an article in a top journal in a given field would be weighted more than an article in a regional journal.

Furthermore, some nations now offer bonuses to scholars who publish in these journals. Pakistani researchers can receive a bonus between $1,000 and $20,000 based on the JIF of the journal in which they publish. Several Chinese research institutes offer bonuses along similar lines (Archambault and Larivière 2009). That, combined with the global pressure to publish in the most prestigious journals, has increased the submission rates for those journals. From 2000 to 2009, *Science* reported a 22% increase in submissions, although the number of papers published did not increase (Franzoni, Scellato, and Stephan 2011). The end result is that both the most prestigious journals and the scholars they use as reviewers now have a much heavier burden of review than they once did. This takes time and resources away from other more productive activities.

In addition, for all practical purposes, the various incentives to scholars to publish in prestigious "international" journals put a premium on English-language journals. One need only look at the lists produced by AERES (2013). Quite obviously, this creates a considerable advantage for scholars who write English well over those who do not, independently of the quality of their work. But the focus on English and on the particular writing style of English-language scholarly journals has an even more insidious effect, especially on scholars in the social sciences and humanities. Because much research in these fields tends to address local or regional issues for whom the audience is not

English speaking, it is almost by definition excluded from publication in "international" journals. Thus, pressure to publish in international journals is tantamount to ignoring issues of local or regional importance. For example, Hanafi (2011, 300) notes, "[t]he 2008 annual report of the Faculty of Arts and Sciences at AUB [American University of Beirut] demonstrates clearly how few social science publications are published in Arabic (only three of 245 articles and two out of 27 books)."

Here, too, other problems arise. In particular, highly prestigious journals tend to have low acceptance rates. Hence, reviewers and editors are likely to be far more orthodox in deciding what to publish. Some years ago, George Akerlof (1970) attempted to publish a paper in the *American Economic Review* that defied contemporary economic thought. Akerlof finally published it in the less prestigious *Quarterly Journal of Economics* (Cassidy 2009). He was later awarded the Nobel Prize in economics largely on the basis of that article. A similar case might be made about Barbara McClintock's brilliant work on "jumping genes." In short, insisting that researchers publish in the most prestigious journals focuses research on the tried and true, on conventional methods and established theories, on puzzle solving rather than asking new questions.

Moreover, with few exceptions, this approach encourages publications in disciplinary journals rather than those that are interdisciplinary. After all, interdisciplinary journals are by definition at the edges of several fields. Hence, they are often unread by those at the "core" of a discipline, and they are certainly regarded by those at the core as less prestigious.

In addition, the JIF is computed using citations *only* from the two previous years. Hence, the JIF for a journal for 2013 would be calculated by summing the citations to articles published in

2011 and 2012. One implication of this is that journals in fields in which citations lag more than two years will have lower impact factors. Because those fields in which papers take more time to be recognized and are less likely to become obsolescent tend to be in social sciences and humanities, journals in these domains of scholarship have lower JIFs.

Finally, there is enormous variation in the importance attributed to articles even within the top journals. A few will be widely cited, used in the revision of research practices, or seen as the model for future research in a given field. However, most will receive few citations and may even be ignored. Hence, publishing an article in a highly prestigious journal in no way says much about the quality of that particular article.

**Downgrading of books and book chapters.** The flip side of the obsession with articles in scholarly journals is the declining incentives to publish either book chapters or books. Without question, many book chapters are invited and not peer reviewed. Similarly, there are many commercial book publishers who will publish with minimal review as long as they see a market for the book in question. But books and book chapters often serve scholarly purposes that are poorly reflected in journal articles. Books and book chapters may bring together in one place the current knowledge about a particular field, serving as a manual for working scholars as well as a guide for neophytes. Books also often allow authors to explore ideas that cannot be examined fully in the limited space of a journal article. Downgrading books and book chapters will have the likely effect of making such reviews and integrative summaries harder to obtain, thereby slowing progress in a given field.

**Competing for grants.** It is of no surprise to anyone reading this that grant competitions have become commonplace in research around the world. In contrast, grants to institutions have diminished in size and frequency, including those established more than a century ago and often known as block grants or formula funds in the world of agricultural research.[2] Proponents of competitive grants, in line with neoliberal claims about markets, argue that competitions ensure that the most promising researchers are funded, irrespective of their institutional affiliations or geographical location. However, most competitive grants—at least as presently constituted—have several major problems associated with them.

*Cost.* Competitions require the development of complex bureaucracies for peer review. This includes both State bureaucracies that administer the grants programs as well as auditing procedures for the institutions receiving the grants as required by funding agencies. At many institutions, as much as one-third to one-half of each grant award goes to so-called indirect costs (i.e., the costs of administering the grant as well as of services that are not directly included in the grant itself such as heat, water, electricity, and library services). Furthermore, the relatively low success rates (in the US context about 20% of submissions, often lower in Britain) mean that much of researchers', graduate students', and staff's time devoted to developing applications is largely wasted. In addition, one survey suggests that US faculty who receive grants spend as much as 42% of their time administering the grant rather than engaged in research (Decker et al. 2007; Rockwell 2009). Another study shows a doubling of administrative time over a 30-year period (Barham, Foltz, and Prager 2014). In short, competitions are costly to administer and have what economists would describe as high transaction costs.

*The Matthew effect.* Initially noted by sociologist Robert Merton (1968), the Matthew effect refers to the lines in the Gospel of Matthew (25:29): "For unto every one that hath shall be given, and he shall have abundance: but from him that hath not shall be taken even that which he hath." In short, those who are already recognized are far more likely to be recognized again. This is particularly true for competitive grants, where those who are already recipients of grants are more likely than others to receive additional grants. Despite attempts by many funding agencies to reverse this process, it continues to a substantial degree, posing significant problems for young researchers who lack a record of support.

*Duration.* Although some research projects can take decades to complete, competitive grants are rarely for periods longer than three years. As a consequence, the shift from block grants to competitive grants makes it difficult or impossible to fund such long-term research. This is especially true of long-term research in fields such as ecology and plant breeding, which cannot be easily divided into small morsels for purposes of grant seeking.

*Geographical situatedness.* Especially in the natural and social sciences, research is geographically situated. For example, unlike most engineering and physical science research, agricultural, forestry, soils, and fisheries research is often regionally specific. Hence, much research of this sort relevant to Norway is not particularly useful to Italy. Occasionally, similar issues appear in the social sciences. For example, qualitative research on social movements must be done at a particular site. Competitive granting mechanisms often fail to take this feature of research into account.

*Grant writing.* Competitive grants tend to reward those persons who are good at grant writing. In many fields, this task is often taken on by senior scholars, whereas junior scholars actually engage in executing the research (Hyde, Clarke, and Drennan 2013). Arguably, the skills required for grant writing are different from those required to engage in research or to write articles for publication. Much as is the case with test taking among students, to some degree grant writing rewards those who are able to demonstrate their skills in grant writing, independent of the value of that research. Of particular note is that grant applications require that the writer of the grant demonstrate the importance of the project to one or another funding agency goal and the superiority of the method(s) used by the proposer to other approaches. At the same time, the applicant must avoid opening up questions that cannot be addressed by the proposed research. Scholars who are good at these skills may be far weaker in executing the grant once it is received.

*Block grants versus competitive grants.* Finally, there is some limited evidence which suggests that block grants are more effective than competitive grants. For example, one study argues that this is the case in the field of agricultural research, at least with respect to its impact on agricultural productivity (Huffman and Evenson 2006). Given the high costs—spread across granting agencies, recipient institutions, and careers of individual scholars—of running competitive grants programs, and their negative consequences noted above, it would appear that the presumption of the alleged superiority of competitive grants would at least require more careful analysis.

**Greater incidence of fraud.** Research fraud may involve a variety of illicit activities, including plagiarism,[3] publishing what are

essentially the same results in several places, conveniently delet-
ing data that contradict the desired results, or fabricating data to
support a given hypothesis. In perhaps the worst instances, it
involves deliberate destruction of data collected by others so
as to discredit their research (see e.g., Maher 2010). All are promoted by the need to excel in various performance audits.

Evidence suggests that fraudulent papers are now far more
common than they were just a few decades ago. Although one
could argue that this rise in the rate of fraud is the result of better
means of detection, more likely it is a consequence of the rising
pressure on scholars to publish. One recent study of 2,047
retracted papers in the biomedical and life sciences found that
misconduct was the reason for retraction in 67% of the cases,
whereas only 21% were retracted due to error (Fang, Steen, and
Casadevall 2012). In addition, the authors noted a tenfold rise in
retractions due to fraud since 1975. All of this undermines the
fundamental trust implicit in peer review processes and
the fabric of scholarly research. Moreover, somewhat ironically,
the usual "solution" posed to fraudulent behavior does not
involve modifying the current market-like reward system but
enhancing training in the responsible conduct of research and
expanding the audit mechanisms (Steneck 2013). Neither
approach addresses the key issue.

**Ghost and honorary authorship.** Ghost authorship consists of
someone writing an article whose name does not appear in the
list of authors. Honorary authorship involves asking someone
well known in a given field to have his name listed as an author,
although that person had little or no connection with the
research in question. In both instances, the intent is to promote
a given product or process through publication in an apparently scholarly and disinterested place. There are now far too

many documented cases of both ghost and honorary authorship of scholarly articles. This is particularly the case when the article in question is seen as having economic value to a given company.

Although there are only a few careful studies of ghost and honorary authorship, what data exist are disturbing. In one recent study of six respected general medical journals, 21% of the published papers had either honorary or ghost authors or both. Moreover, this number was lower than that reported in 1996, before the problem was well identified (Wislar et al. 2011). Whether these estimates apply to other fields is simply not known, but it is certainly likely to be an issue in other disciplines, especially those where companies value particular research outcomes and the imprimatur of key figures in the field.

**Forced citations by journal editors.** Because journals as well as researchers are now often ranked by citation counts and many research organizations reward researchers who publish in highly ranked journals, some journal editors have begun to promote their journals by putting pressure on authors to cite papers previously published in their journals.[4] This means that papers only marginally related to a given published paper are now to be found in the list of references. In addition, because review articles tend to be cited more frequently than others, editors anxious to raise their journal's place in the rankings can increase the journal space devoted to reviews. Moreover, some journal editors have promoted their journals by publishing editorials in which they cite most of the articles published in that same journal. Of course, it is difficult to determine how widespread this problem is given that one needs "insider" information about a particular journal's policies to accurately analyze whether journal self-citation is the result of authors' citation patterns or editorial pressure.

Moreover, regardless of how widespread forced citations are, they have little effect on the rankings among journals, in large part, because of the importance accorded to the "top" journals' reputations. This forms a vicious circle. Given the budgetary limits of library subscriptions and the rising cost of journals, librarians try to avoid subscribing to journals that are read by few scholars. As noted above, they do this through the use of indexes such as the Web of Science. In addition, because scholars rarely read certain journals, they also rarely if ever cite them. If only a few scholars cite them, then indexes do not list them. In fact, even if an excellent article is published in a journal that is not indexed, it is unlikely to be read or cited. Furthermore, most editors and reviewers do not wish to spend their time editing or reviewing for a journal that rarely attracts high-quality papers (Edlin and Rubinfeld 2004).

This has important consequences for heterodox views in various disciplines. For example, Jakob Kapeller (2010) has shown how authors who publish in orthodox economics journals rarely cite others outside the discipline. In contrast, authors who publish in heterodox economics journals frequently cite those outside their field. Of course, the orthodox economists are far greater in number than the heterodox ones, and the orthodox journals are more frequently cited overall. Therefore, it is extremely difficult for a journal that publishes heterodox views to attract sufficient citations in orthodox journals to be indexed, let alone to rise in the journal rankings. Likely, what Kapeller found for economics is true in other disciplines as well.

**Rising costs of journals as a few publishers corner the market.** In part as a result of the pressure to publish as well as the ranking of journals, today a handful of companies publish most of the major academic journals listed in the Web of Science. One recent study of concentration in journal publishing examined all the journals indexed in *Journal Citation Reports* from 1997 to 2009. The study found that 0.2% of the publishers produced 50% of the journals and articles. They also noted a trend toward increasing concentration. Whereas 22 publishers produced 50% of the journals in 1997, by 2009, that number had declined to 7 (Didegah and Gazni 2011). At the same time, library subscription prices have risen dramatically (Edlin and Rubinfeld 2004, 120).

The publishers make their money by (1) requiring that authors surrender their rights to the publication in question, and (2) asking reviewers to comment on those papers at no cost to publishers. This made sense when most journals were published by professional societies or academic presses; today that is no longer the case. Instead, publishers sell the results of their endeavors to libraries and the general public at what are often exorbitant fees. Indeed, in 2010, Elsevier—one of the largest scholarly publishers with more than 16% of the market—reported profits of 36% on revenues of $3.2 billion (Gusterson 2012).

**Conflicts of interest in research.** Not too long ago, most public universities and research institutes were careful about what private funds to accept and under what conditions. For example, in 1931, a director of an American agricultural experiment station (then the organizations receiving the lion's share of public funding) noted, "In accepting monies from industry, the station director must always keep in mind that such monies should have for their first purpose the upbuilding of agriculture used in the broadest sense. We should not use our station facilities for the promotion of merely private gain" (Russell 1931, 226).

However, in recent years, university scientists in many nations have been encouraged to collaborate with scientists in the private sector, even going so far as to launch joint ventures. In addition, while earlier collaborations involved just a few scientists, more recent collaborations have involved entire departments or centers. The Novartis–University of California Berkeley agreement was one such institutional collaboration. Although neither the worst fears of detractors (selling the university to the private sector) nor the high expectations of supporters (great scientific advances) were realized, the overall impact was to undermine the reputation of the department and the university in many quarters (Rudy et al. 2007).

Furthermore, many universities and some research institutes have established research parks on the edges of campus so as to encourage greater interaction between public and private researchers. Although in principle there is nothing problematic about such research parks, the devil is always in the details. In some cases, this simply permits firms to be near departments where researchers have similar interests. In other cases, it promotes overly close relations, thereby undermining both the independence of public researchers and putting barriers in place for other firms. In the worst instances, such close relations between public institutions and private firms leads to the suppression of critical voices, as was the case at one Canadian university (see page 103).

In addition, some disciplines have become so closely associated with particular industries that it is hard to find scholars who are not receiving some sort of industry support. Food science and nutrition departments are emblematic of this problem.

As Marion Nestle (quoted in Warren and Nestle 2010) has noted, "soft-drink companies such as Coca-Cola and PepsiCo lose no opportunity to sponsor professional meetings; provide training positions; send free samples and technical materials; and support professional newsletters, teaching materials, and journals." Moreover, she notes that most independent studies clearly link childhood obesity with soft drink consumption, whereas those sponsored by industry dispute this claim.

Similarly, pharmaceutical companies only fund research on drugs of interest to the firm. They also frequently provide travel money to researchers whose findings support use of the drug being promoted. In addition, they may pay selected researchers who agree to serve as honorary authors (Mirowski 2011). When used by agencies that approve drugs for general use, such practices make it possible for potentially dangerous drugs to be approved. Even projects approved by Institutional Review Boards usually fail to reveal these issues because they are designed to protect subjects in research projects, not to ensure that no conflicts of interest exist.

Conflicts of interest may also exist when supposedly disinterested scholars serve on standards setting committees, a common practice for many standards development organizations. Such organizations set standards for a wide variety of physical objects, industrial processes, and "best practices." If the scholars who serve have industry ties, at least the appearance of a conflict of interest is in place.

Such conflicts of interest may also exist when researchers consult for so-called "expert network firms." These companies seek out the top academic researchers in a given field and link them with companies willing to pay for their expertise. They then receive phone calls from those companies asking about ongoing research projects and programs. In some instances, such researchers have stepped over the line and become involved in insider-trading schemes, as either active participants or informants giving away corporate secrets. So risky is this kind of consulting that the prestigious Cleveland Clinic has forbidden its staff to enroll in expert networks (Mervis 2013).

What all this means is that a large and growing portion of scholars in public institutions are no longer disinterested. Instead, they are linked to those who advocate particular positions on various issues of concern to both the scholarly community and the general public to advance their personal or institutional market-driven goals. Therefore, conflicts of interest have become a major problem in journal article reviewing and publication, debates about various issues of public policy, and submission and reviewing of research grants. For example, one study of some 94 articles reporting health risks and nutritional value of genetically modified crops found that financial or professional conflicts of interest were commonplace when negative findings were reported (Diels et al. 2011).

**Changes in intellectual property rights.** Markets can only exist when objects or processes are considered as saleable property. One way to create markets where they did not exist before is to expand intellectual property rights (IPRs). Clearly, in capitalist societies, certain activities become so unprofitable without IPRs as to be abandoned. Hence, some sort of copyright and patent protection is necessary if there is to be any *monetary* incentive to engage in or reproduce creative work at all. Furthermore, openly releasing certain products and processes leads to the orphan drug problem. Specifically, if a product or process for which there is little demand is released to the general public, there may be an insufficient monetary incentive for any particular company to invest in its development and sale. This is particularly the case for products such as specialized drugs for rare diseases. Without a patent, no pharmaceutical company will produce the drug for fear that some other company will do the same and undercut them on the price. Similar issues appear for improved varieties of minor crops.

However, over the last several decades, IPRs have been greatly expanded. There are now IPRs for organisms, seeds, research tools and instruments, computer software, and a variety of other domains. The expansion of IPRs has had a number of consequences for university research.

*Open versus proprietary knowledge.* The entire academic enterprise is built on the notion that knowledge should be freely available. As economists rightly note, most knowledge is nonrival and nonexclusive; anyone can use it without depleting the stock of knowledge for others. We academics speak of "contributions to the literature," where a contribution is a gift to the discipline or research field as well as to the larger society.

In contrast, the private sector values proprietary knowledge, for which erecting barriers to use of that knowledge (e.g., trade secrets, patents, copyrights, steep learning curves) enhances profitability. The expansion of IPRs shifts the boundaries between scholarly research and private gain. In consequence, in the biological sciences especially, "materials transfer agreements" have become commonplace. Such agreements both slow down the spread of knowledge and block researchers from engaging in certain kinds of experiments. In the most egregious examples, university researchers find their research projects tied in knots as various organizations have IPRs that relate to different parts of their research agenda. This creates what some have called an "anti-commons" (i.e., a situation in which each advance requires that one obtain [purchase?] permission from other persons or firms) (Heller and Eisenberg 1998). In addition, the tendency toward granting patents on genes sharply reduces their use by both medical practitioners and plant scientists (Berthels, Matthijs, and Van Overwalle 2011).

*Engaging in research about protected innovations.* Once something is protected by IPRs, researchers often find themselves denied access to that innovation even for purposes of research. For example, purchasers of genetically modified seeds must sign an agreement barring their use in research. Technically, they do not purchase them at all but only "lease" them for one season. Scientists who wish to do research on the environmental consequences of such crops must get corporate approval, which can be both limited (in terms of what research can be done and what information can be published) and agonizingly slow. Whether this restriction is legal is unclear, but it has had a chilling effect on public research. As a result, a few years ago, a group of scientists wrote a letter of protest to the US Environmental Protection Agency about their inability to examine the environmental effects of genetically modified plants (Pollack 2009). As they feared reprisals by the companies involved, they initially requested anonymity. Later, a subset of them published a paper outlining their concerns and expressing their hope that a recent agreement with the American Seed Trade Association would bring about a resolution (Sappington et al. 2010). However, it is still unclear whether the agreement has had the desired effect (Stutz 2010).

*The rise of IP offices on university campuses.* Since the passage of the Bayh-Dole Act (PL 96–517), US universities have been encouraged to patent inventions developed with government funds. Similar events have taken place in Canada (Martin and Ouellet 2010). As a result, most large research universities have formed intellectual property offices. A few have benefitted enormously as they have been able to obtain license fees from patents on extremely lucrative inventions. However, the tail on the distribution of revenues from patents is extremely long. One or two patents may generate nearly all of the revenues accumulated by a single university. Hence, although a few universities have benefitted, far more have found their intellectual property offices to be large sinkholes. After all, most things that are patentable are of little or no economic value.

Perhaps more important, it is at least questionable whether IP offices serve the public good. A recent US National Research Council report, for example, tells us that "[t]he first goal of university technology transfer involving IP is the expeditious and wide dissemination of university-generated technology for the public good" (Merrill and Mazza 2010, 2). It also warns university officials that IP offices should not be seen as revenue sources but as one more means for promoting the public good. One can hardly object to this. However, it is an open secret that universities do see IP offices as potential cash cows and try as best as possible to maximize the returns on their "investments." In Canada, that has been encouraged by the national and provincial governments, although it has been singularly unsuccessful (Martin and Ouellet 2010).

Yet the expansion of IPRs and the embracing of them as a source of revenue show how inappropriate this model is for university research. As Simon Marginson (2011, 8) explains,

This peculiar, public good-laden character of knowledge helps to explain why universities have been consistently disappointed in their expectations of commercial returns to research. ... There are normally several steps that must occur before ideas become enfolded into commodities, and by that stage the ideas have long been transformed by other economic processes in which the commercial value is created. It takes deep pockets to hold onto private ownership of the idea in itself all the way down the commercial value-creating chain.

Hence, to date, only a few universities have been able to turn IPRs into a significant source of commercial returns on investment. Universities are ill prepared to become venture capitalists. With few exceptions, they lack the capital, the enthusiasm for economic returns (in contrast to increased status or prestige), and the forms of organization necessary to move from knowledge to objects or processes that do well in the marketplace.

*Rewarding IPRs.* Yet encouraging faculty to produce knowledge that is subject to IPRs shifts the reward system for scholars. In addition to including intellectual property as a criterion for merit increases, at many universities and research institutes, a significant share of the royalties on intellectual property are given to the inventor. Arguably, this shifts the boundaries between knowledge as a public good and knowledge as a private good. Especially in the sciences and engineering, faculty have become perhaps all too attuned to the lure of producing patentable inventions, to the detriment of those who may benefit society but have no immediate economic payoff.

In short, the expansion of IPRs has had the (intended) effect of enclosing parts of the commons. As a result, many scientists at public universities and research institutes have shifted their research agendas so as to pursue an elusive monetary prize. It is unclear how differently knowledge might have developed were

IPRs to have remained more limited in scope. Yet it is clear that the expansion of IPRs has not been particularly profitable for most universities.

*** 

In summary, at universities and research institutes in many nations, there is little doubt that, at least for permanent faculty, merit increases, promotion, and tenure are focused heavily on research publications to the virtual exclusion of all else. Education and public engagement are seen as of lesser importance, but also other faculty activities that are essential to the university are downgraded—advising students, attending seminars, organizing professional meetings, reviewing articles and grant applications, and informal interactions with other faculty members. Kathleen Lynch (2006, 9) put the matter even more strongly: "Once academics are only assessed and rewarded for communicating with other academics that is all they will do. In a research assessment system where one is rewarded for publishing in peer-reviewed books and journals, there is little incentive to invest in teaching, even the teaching that is part of one's job. The incentive to teach or disseminate findings in the public sphere through public lectures, dialogues or partnerships with relevant civil society or statutory bodies is negligible."

In short, the roles of researchers tend to be narrowed as they are individualized (i.e., focused more and more on generating the next peer-reviewed publication, itself often a highly individualizing activity). Such individualization often comes at the detriment to students, colleagues, and the public.

## Public Engagement and Extension

Although doubtless there is some truth to the image of universities as "ivory towers," many universities and research institutes have to varying degrees been linked to various publics, either through ongoing debates about societal issues in which both scholars and members of the general public took part or by virtue of close links between certain (local or national) publics and the research underway. Arguably, in the modern world, these linkages between the scholarly world and that of practitioners have been most visible and well developed in the domain of agriculture.

Domestically, as nation-states began to develop in Europe, this initially took the form of attempts to promote the use of medicinal crops and the acclimatization of exotic plants in botanical gardens. Later, they began to promote growth in agricultural productivity. Hence, most agricultural research was from its inception seen as a State activity designed to promote the health and welfare of the population, as well as to maintain political stability by ensuring that food was cheap and abundant.

In contrast, to enhance colonial commerce, it first took the form of botanical gardens that served as plant transfer stations, often valorizing imperial ambitions. Plants of economic value found in one colony could be tested in the gardens and then transferred to other colonies enhancing the value of those colonies to the "mother country." The *Jardin des Plantes* in Paris and the Kew Gardens in Britain remain as testimony to these policies.

Today, in a world in which few colonies continue to exist, nearly every nation has some sort of agricultural experiment station where research on crops, livestock, forestry, and/or fisheries is conducted at public expense. Many of these experiment stations and gardens are also involved in education of both the next generation of scientists and a wide range of practitioners.

Furthermore, nearly all of these gardens and experiment stations have at some time engaged in or were linked to some form of extension services, designed to interact with farmers and other persons involved in agriculture broadly conceived. Given the longevity of these relations with various publics in the agricultural sector as well as their ubiquity, their fate under neoliberalism can be seen to be emblematic of the changing relations between research institutes and universities and the publics they claim to serve.

**Decline in public support.** Arguably even more than in education and research, there has been a decline in interest in and financial support for interaction with the various publics that are or might be interested in dialogues with scholars at universities and research institutes. This is particularly the case with respect to the agricultural sector, where research has been linked to agricultural production for more than a century (Harwood 2012). Some of this is the result of the decline in the size of the farm population and their political clout. In addition, the obsession with research publication has in many places made dialogue with publics at best an afterthought. Part of it is also extension's difficulty in adapting to a rapidly changing potential clientele that might include environmentalists and consumer advocates as well as technologically sophisticated corporate farms. Indeed, since its inception, extension has tended to promote new technologies on the farm and in the home, and to avoid more clearly controversial issues such as the role of farm labor, conflicts within the agricultural sector, and both rural and urban poverty.

**Growth of private extension-like services.** From a neoliberal perspective, extension services involve unnecessary and undesirable interference in what otherwise would be a flourishing market in agricultural services. Hence, extension has been particularly squeezed financially in recent years as private services have begun to flourish. However, privatization of extension services has its costs as those without the ability to pay are squeezed out of the newly formed market and the nature of the knowledge imparted shifts. This is true for both the activities formerly promoted by extension as well as similar services provided by other public agencies (Lave, Doyle, and Robertson 2010).

**Wider gap between research and extension.** Although the model of "the researcher shooting an arrow into the extension agent who shoots it into a farmer" (Bunting 1979) is both empirically mistaken and theoretically bankrupt, it was certainly the case in the past that extension agents generally accepted the innovations developed by researchers and worked to convince farmers to use them. In contrast, today much public agricultural research cannot be used directly by farmers; instead, it is used largely by agribusiness firms, which then market that research in the form of products to farmers.

**Decline of public interest research.** Although there certainly were no halcyon days of public sector research, public universities and research institutes were established based on the claim that they served the public good. Agricultural research, among the first scientific domains to receive State support, is a case in point. Much of the research produced by agricultural experiment stations involved changing practices rather than developing material technologies. Hence, research focused on improving (agri)cultural and farm management practices. When material objects were produced, they were often in the form of improved seeds; such seeds were largely varietals that could be reproduced by farmers who typically engaged in seed saving. However, such public interest science brings few if any market benefits. After all, in most instances, the results of the research were and remain freely available to anyone who is interested. The decline of research on biological (as opposed to chemical) control of undesired insect pests is a case in point (Warner et al. 2011). The former results in knowledge freely available to all, whereas the latter creates proprietary knowledge available to those who can afford to pay for it. What is true in agriculture is largely true in other domains as well.

**Rise of strongly ideological think tanks.** Think tanks and foundations such as the *Association pour la liberté économique et le progrès social* (France), the Institute for Economic Affairs (UK), or the Heritage Foundation, the Cato Institute, and the American Enterprise Institute (US), often financed by wealthy donors and large corporations, now compete with scholars at public universities and research institutes to engage various publics and develop policies of all kinds. Many of them are connected through the Atlas Network, a project of the Atlas Economic Research Foundation (2013) "connecting a global network of more than 400 free-market organizations in over 80 countries to the ideas and resources needed to advance the cause of liberty." Nearly all of these organizations promote market and market-like solutions to all sorts of problems. Lacking a need to connect and often hostile to academic scholarship, they have been far more effective than academics at developing materials for consumption by the general public.

They have also been highly successful in promoting agnotology (Proctor and Schiebinger 2008) (i.e., spreading doubt about anything and anyone who challenges the notion that all problems can be addressed through the market). Hence, they have vigorously attacked those persons and organizations concerned about cigarette smoking, global climate change, the hole in the ozone, acid rain, and a host of other environmental issues. They have even attacked long-deceased Rachel Carson, author of *Silent Spring*, for allegedly causing the deaths of thousands of persons.

These think tanks and foundations have used three complementary approaches to agnotology. First, they have worked hard to spread doubt, knowing full well that no scholarly work is ever so certain that it cannot be challenged. Second, and perhaps of greatest concern, they have argued that as self-interested isolates, scientists desire to maximize their human capital and will do anything to promote their views, gain more funding, and increase their salaries and prestige. Hence, the rise in the number of fraudulent papers and other scientific misconduct as a result of New Public Management is "proof" that scientists are merely self-interested. This conveniently gives greater credence to the neoliberal think tanks. Finally, they have argued that the crises noted above are relatively trivial and that addressing them would not require vast (public) outlays.

Moreover, they have invented slogans such as "sound science" and "junk science" to defame their opponents. In addition, they have been actively involved in the publication of a variety of books, pseudo-scientific journals, and reports that claim to show the falsity of widely accepted scientific conclusions. Indeed, "[a] recent academic study found that of the fifty-six 'environmentally skeptical' books published [in the US] in the 1990s, 92 percent were linked to these right-wing foundations" (Oreskes and Conway 2010, 236).

Nor have these challenges to universities and research institutes been limited to the natural sciences. Those in the social sciences, humanities, and arts have also been subject to attack. In particular, there have been concerted efforts to reduce or eliminate social science and humanities funding, starting with the US National Endowment for the Arts in the 1980s. More recently, neoliberals have attacked social science research in the US Congress, arguing that much of it is irrelevant to national priorities (Weigel 2013).

## Consequences

The changes noted above in administration, education, research, and public engagement have not been without consequences. Although higher education and research were hardly in perfect shape before the so-called reforms began, those reforms pose new problems and threaten to undermine not only the roles of universities and public research institutes but the very idea of a university. They also reduce the ability of such institutions to respond to the crises before us. Among the most serious consequences are the following.

**Higher education is being rapidly altered.** The changes in higher education that have been enacted in much of the world have already transformed what it means to be educated. Instead of encouraging inquiry, creativity, and intellectual curiosity, far too much of university education now consists of rote memorization of "facts" that will be obsolete within a decade or less. Moreover, instead of producing educated citizens, we are more and more producing trained workers who will be able to perform competently in a given job, but who will be utterly unprepared for future disruptions, technical change, or political upheaval. Moreover, as noted above, in an effort to increase student "satisfaction," we are rapidly reducing expectations for student achievement.

**Research is more and more dominated by immediate (often economic) ends.** Instead of asking whether the research in question furthers our understanding of the world, or how it might promote some public good, research is increasingly evaluated based on its estimated (market) value—even before it is started. For example, several US research granting agencies now ask grant applicants to discuss the "broader impacts" of the grant. Doing so requires the applicant to describe in the most optimistic economic, political, and social terms what might occur were the research to be funded and completely successful; of course, were that knowledge available, the research would already have been completed.

Moreover, there is considerable irony in judging research in terms of future impact. On the one hand, it is nearly impossible to forecast all the consequences of successful upstream research. Who, for example, expected the global Internet to emerge out of a computer communications project developed by the US Defense Department? Who expected genetic screening to emerge from the discovery of the double helix? Who could have predicted that the development of lasers would have led to DVDs? On the other hand, even the most applied research may not be successfully implemented until a wide range of other conditions are met.

Consider, for example, the case of Oliver Evans who invented the "steam car" in 1785 (Bathe and Bathe 1935). Although it worked, roads were generally in poor condition, service stations were lacking, fuel could not be purchased easily, and the steering mechanism was awkward at best. It took another century to put all these pieces together and develop what we know today as automobiles. Similarly, the standard shipping container was conceived of some 30 years before it was in widespread use (Levinson 2006). Its use was hampered by, among other things, (1) the lack of an agreed-upon standard that would accommodate ships, trucks, and trains; (2) the lack of standard means for fastening containers for transport; (3) inadequate port facilities; (4) inadequate equipment for hoisting containers; and (5) a lack of ships designed for them. Like most inventions, these required an entire infrastructure of changes for their success. In short, in an ironic way, the demand for a narrow focus on immediate ends may actually undermine precisely the kinds of research that lead to breakthroughs in our overall knowledge of the world as well as the development of entirely new industries.

**Increasing corporate domination of the research enterprise.** In the domains of food and agriculture, as well as pharmaceuticals and energy, the public sector is dwarfed by private research expenditures. In agriculture in the past, there was a division of labor, with the private sector focused largely on machines and chemicals and the public sector focused largely on biological, environmental, and social sciences. In just a few decades, this has shifted; the private sector now dominates all technical aspects of agricultural research. By 2000, more than half of all agricultural research expenditures in the OECD countries were made by the private sector (Fuglie et al. 2012). Moreover, virtually all agricultural input industries are dominated by a handful of large firms that tend to focus on a small number of widely produced commodities. These firms appear able to block market entry in a variety of ways as well as to channel innovation in ways that serve their ends. In addition, much public sector research now must go through these same corporations to reach stakeholders. Hence, much of the research agenda is now firmly in the hands of the private sector.

The situation in pharmaceuticals is similar. Governments around the world support medical research that ultimately results in the creation of new pharmaceutical products. But the public often pays twice for those pharmaceuticals—first in taxes to support public research and again in handsome profits to pharmaceutical companies. In addition, the focus on curative as opposed to preventive medicine and on drugs rather than diet, exercise, and other therapies supports the pharmaceutical companies' agenda. Whether it effectively supports the public good is another question.

Indeed, in the United Kingdom (UK), the Economic and Social Research Council, the UK's funding agency for social science research, has made its first "strategic priority," "Economic Performance and Sustainable Growth." Similarly, "Business Engagement" is to be promoted and is seen as having no downside (Economic and Social Research Council n.d.). As noted in one PowerPoint presentation: "Business/private sector [is] a priority for increased engagement. [We] aim to increase business co-funding to 5% of external income by 2015." In short, not only has funding shifted toward unvarnished support for the private sector; the private sector is invited to become part of the social science granting process, thereby signaling that research critical of the private sector is unwelcome.

**Discouraging innovation and high-risk research.** Many of the changes noted above serve to discourage innovation and high-risk research. After all, constant auditing of researchers requires that one continually churn out a more or less even flow of research products. Engaging in highly innovative or high-risk research tends to threaten that flow of products because it goes beyond puzzle solving to revolutionary (Kuhn 1970) or even post-normal (Funtowicz and Ravetz 1993) science. For example, Fleming's discovery of penicillin and McClintock's discovery of "jumping genes" took many years before they were recognized by the scholarly community (Kumar 2010). In contrast, much contemporary genomic research involves contributing to the development of massive databases but rarely goes beyond that. Similarly, negative results are now more rarely published than several decades ago. As Fanelli (2011, 1) argues, "[m]ethodological artefacts cannot explain away these patterns, which support the hypotheses that research is becoming less pioneering and/or that the objectivity with which results are produced and published is decreasing."

**The university as a growth machine.** University faculty and administrators have been more and more encouraged by legislators and government officials to assume the role of a growth machine (cf. Molotch 1976). Imagining the world as one gigantic competition among nations, corporations, and individuals, universities are to assume their role not as generators of new knowledge for the public good, but as generators of economic development based on new, generally proprietary, knowledge. This shift in the focus of universities has rarely had the expected payoff and has deprived us of the public goods that universities might actually deliver.

**Isolated scholars and organizational solidarity.** The combination of treating scholars as autonomous individuals who wish to maximize their human capital and imposing New Public Management so as to avoid the allegedly widespread moral hazard posed by those same scholars has led to a rise in insecurity and uncertainty in universities and research institutes. On the one hand, it has led to the imposition of a much greater degree of hierarchy. Administrators must now justify both their own positions as well as those of their organization in market terms. Hence, in imposing New Public Management, they have substantially increased their control within both universities and research institutes. In many such institutions, scholarly and professional self-governance is at best a sham and at worst nonexistent. Moreover, "[a]s faculty time is diverted into non-academic activities, the university is less and less able to produce the substantive outputs and values—teaching and research—that generate revenue for the institution" (Barrow 2010, 334).

On the other hand, administrators have been given the thankless role of promoting loyalty to the university or research institute, even as scholars find themselves more and more isolated and insecure. What is rarely asked is why scholars, who are apparently not to be trusted and entirely focused on salary increases, should remain loyal to their increasingly hierarchical employers. Put differently, as the democratic and professional features of universities and research institutes are undermined, why should scholars remain loyal to organizations over which they have little or no control?

***

Although it might be argued that none of these changes is sufficiently large to undermine the notion of a university or public research institute, together they make a formidable combination. In particular, they have the effect of challenging the notions of scholarship and academic freedom essential for public research worthy of the name. They do this not so much through outright censorship, although that certainly occurs occasionally—and has occurred as long as universities and research institutes have been around as institutions—but through subtle yet profound changes in what shall count as scholarship, education, research, and public engagement. For example, the central focus on entrepreneurialism among scholars promotes those whose work lends itself to an entrepreneurial career—securing grants, publishing in "top" journals, patenting inventions, starting new businesses, and providing research results that have immediate economic value. Note also that the pressure to secure extramural competitive grants, which as former US President Dwight D. Eisenhower warned us[1] always comes with strings attached, shifts faculty away from those forms of research that require little or no additional funding. Indeed, as Normand Baillargeon (2011, 45) observes, "... one cannot (and it is so much the better) obtain a grant to read Plato, to study Dewey (Box 5), to understand the concept of indoctrination or to meditate on what the fact of education signifies." This certainly includes many projects in the social sciences, arts, and humanities, but it also includes many studies in the sciences that require minimal instrumentation such as those of natural history.

A case in point is the biotechnology research agreement reached by Monsanto and the University of Manitoba (Canada). The university negotiated a C\$7 million 10-year lease with Monsanto to form a Crop Technology Center on campus. No discussion was held with the faculty about this decision to the dismay of many faculty members. Then for three years, the university tried (ultimately unsuccessfully) to suppress the release of a film critical of agricultural biotechnologies (Peekhaus 2010).

Similarly, the pressure to publish in the "top" journals limits scholars to projects that are within the intellectual range of

**Box 5**
**John Dewey**

John Dewey (1859–1952) was a pragmatist philosopher, perhaps best known for his views on education (e.g., Dewey 1961 [1916], 1962 [1902, 1915]). He believed education was essential to the maintenance of a democratic society as it informed public opinion. Dewey rejected the idea that schools were solely about teaching content and skills; for him they were places in which to realize one's full potential and contribute to the public good. That meant learning about both subject matter and values. To do this, students were to participate in the curriculum by relating content to their prior experiences. Therefore, as much as possible, learning was to be active much as it is in civic life, building on the differing experiences and abilities of students. In other words, instead of being lectured to about the facts, students were to be encouraged to figure out for themselves how the social and natural worlds were constructed as well as what place certain values held for society. In doing so, they would become critical thinkers, constantly asking questions about how things might be improved.

For Dewey, education, like science, was about experiment and experience. Hence, he argued that education should be organized such that students could learn for themselves, with teachers acting as guides rather than authorities. In addition, schools would be treated as laboratories so as to determine how best to prepare students for life in a democratic society.

Moreover, Dewey did not merely write about these issues. He was actively engaged in experimenting with educational reforms at the University of Chicago Laboratory School. His work and practice strongly influenced American education from kindergarten through the university.

those journals. At the same time, it demotes those faculty members who value knowledge that does not lead to these ends, but rather leads to, for example, greater insights into the human condition, more critical thinking, greater cross-cultural understanding, or new practices that practitioners in various fields can adopt without having to pay for them. As one British observer notes, "In this now quasi-official view of the university, research and teaching that do not serve business or wealth creation are seen as luxuries; and it is equally assumed that luxuries should not be funded from the public purse" (Docherty 2012, 50).

Similarly, in the domain of formal education, the overvaluing of science and engineering disciplines brings with it the undervaluing of everything else. Science and engineering are paradoxically and inaccurately claimed to have a direct positive effect on *everyone's* well-being, whereas the arts, humanities, and social sciences are seen as merely decorative and ancillary options that may be dispensed with when funds are short. Indeed, England has made this point painfully clear in the recent neoliberal reforms described above. This, combined with the decline of overall public support for universities and the placing of enormous debt burdens on students in many nations, sends the word out quite clearly: If you want to succeed in life, if you want to pay off your debts, then enter the sciences or engineering and avoid the arts, humanities, and social sciences.

Furthermore, all of this fails to note that values—a central concern of the humanities and social sciences—occupy a central place in the technosciences. Values motivate researchers to pursue certain paths, help them to decide whether evidence is sufficiently solid to draw inferences, and determine which innovations are embraced and rejected. Thus, for example, thoughtful engineers know that inventions are never neutral with respect to their effects. What is seen as an advance to some is always seen as a retreat by others. Hence, difficult questions of value are right at the core of engineering. Although a given engineer may choose to ignore these value questions, they are embedded in the practice of engineering. For example, a new cultivar that increases per hectare productivity of a crop is likely to also reduce prices. Hence, those farmers not able to increase the area of land in the improved variety will earn less, even as farmers who increase their holdings will keep their incomes the same and consumers will benefit from lower prices. Understanding such complex issues requires more than a technical understanding of various products and processes; it requires a broad base of education that includes the arts, humanities, and social sciences.

***

In summary, in each facet of higher education and research, adoption of neoliberal approaches has largely failed. It has not led to greater efficiencies but to more bureaucracy. It has not led to greater liberties but to more constraints on teaching, research, and engagement. It has not led to more robust and autonomous institutions but to weakened institutions linked too closely to the immediate concerns of the day. It has not led to new ways to grapple with the crises that face us but to treading farther down the same paths that created those crises. Is there a way forward? It is to that issue that I now turn.

## Can Our Universities and Research Institutes Address These Crises?

Here at the beginning of the 21st century, those of us concerned about the future of universities and research institutes are faced with two interrelated and overlapping questions. First, what kinds of universities and research institutes do we want? Second, how can these institutions grapple with the wicked problems facing us? Moreover, we need to ask these questions as they relate to administration, education, research, and public engagement.

**What kinds of universities and research institutes do we want?** This question has been asked thousands of times by faculty members, administrators, students, and others. But note that it requires a double answer. On the one hand, we need to provide (at least tentative) answers about the kind of institutions we want to construct. We must ask what goals we should pursue, what publics we should serve, and what consequences we should have. But we cannot answer that question without also asking what kind of faculty, what kind of public engagement, and what kind of students we should have. This is not merely a matter of fulfilling the wishes of our faculty, our students, or the general public. Were that the case, our job would be easier but far less challenging. To the contrary, answering these questions involves asking what kind of possibilities for changing the selves of faculty, students, and external stakeholders we might collectively wish to pursue. Answering that question involves the creation of learning communities (Fink 2003), in which selves and societies are transformed together through dialogue rather than hierarchy. Learning communities are places where groups of people—faculty, students, staff—come together to learn. They involve learning as a communal process because it is only through communities that knowledge is created and validated.

**How can we grapple with the wicked problems facing us?** Answering this question requires that we reinvent both research and higher education. We need not merely to inquire into the current division of knowledge, but *inquire into how to inquire* about the division of knowledge; not merely to ask how to design incentives for students, for faculty, and for institutions, but *what form(s) of incentives* will be effective in preparing a common future for all; not merely what students should learn, but *how to foster learning communities* for everyone; not merely how to foster democratic ideals through our institutions of higher education, but *how to make those democratic ideals relevant* to the needs and demands of the 21st century. In summary, universities and research institutions must be remade as places where the future is neither already made in the mold of the market nor in which the market is to be avoided at all costs, but where many possible futures are proposed, debated, and opened for discussion by all citizens.

# Remembrance of Things Future: Some Specific Proposals for Change

Devising proposals for change is difficult as one must try to avoid a variety of pitfalls that await anyone attempting to do this. First, given the wide range of issues facing universities and research institutes under various neoliberalisms, what may work in one setting may well fail in another. One size fits all is not an option. Second, one must avoid the temptation to universalize what is in fact local and/or time-bound. Third, language puts limits on what we consider reasonable or possible, yet there is no way to escape the confines of language (Castoriadis 1998 [1975]). Fourth, no one set of alternatives is likely to be acceptable and enactable everywhere; much as there are neoliberalisms, there will also be multiple forms of alternatives. Finally, no set of proposals can claim to be complete. Doubtless, there are other options, other imaginaries, and other means of transforming universities and research institutes that I have failed to recognize.

That said, we might consider three complementary strategies pursued simultaneously. First, we need to develop means to resist neoliberal policies and practices. We need to document and publicize the gross failures of neoliberal policies, not only in our own nations but globally. We need to show how the obsession with markets and competitions results in both wide-spread gaming of the system, working to the (nearly always inadequate) measure, as well as outcomes far removed from even the neoliberals' notions of what is desirable. We need to emphasize how governing at a distance, so-called public–private partnerships, and the outsourcing of government services results not in more efficiency in the provision of public goods, but in the creation of corporate lobbies that promote (often hidden) subsidies for contractors, fire sales of public goods, and promotion of ineffective public services. We need to show how, instead of promoting liberty, as proponents claim, neoliberal reforms promote corporate dominance even as they undermine democratic governance. We need to show the general public how neoliberalism is not so much an alternative to the now defunct and discredited Soviet system, but rather the mirror image of that system.

Second, we need to learn from the neoliberals. We need to learn from their tactics for instituting new policies, enacting new practices, and engaging in dialogue over what policies work best. We need to form alliances with like-minded groups and begin a continuing dialogue over how to end, refashion, abandon, or otherwise derail neoliberal policies. We need to learn to use crises—including the current crises of banking and neoliberal national governments—as opportunities. We need to push past the simplistic neoliberal claim that once markets are constructed, they necessarily have certain properties. We need to show that, because markets and competitions are con-structed, they can be designed to maximize efficiency, but also to maximize the seller's (or buyer's) profits or to promote sus-tainability, energy efficiency, social equity, and many other agreed-on goals.

Finally, we need to create new imaginaries; we need to imagine our collective futures differently from the neoliberals. It is not enough to simply reject neoliberal policies and enactments and demand a return to some romanticized past time. We must break the cycle, the dialectic, and imagine different futures where markets are merely one among many forms that institutions can take, where security, equality, and freedom are once again linked together, where there is not only more democracy but different forms of democracy, where there is a more educated—not merely a better trained—populace, where the exhausted, tired old dichotomies collapse. Where market and state, ideal and material, nature and culture, capitalism and socialism, equality and liberty, are no longer enacted as opposing poles, but as complex networks of ever-changing sociotechnical relations. In short, as Dominique Pestre (2007, 47) argues, "In democratic societies, there exists… a multiplicity of forms of justice among which we should admit there is little compatibility; this variety is also a founding principle of democracy and should be preserved—by preserving a diversity of regulations." With all this in mind, consider the following proposals.

**Make universities and research institutes (more) secure places.** Quite obviously, security must be provided in the sense of protection against violence. But beyond that, today's universities and research institutes at times seem almost designed to produce insecurity. In some nations, students find themselves saddled with enormous debts that take years to repay. Permanent faculty members and researchers find themselves incessantly ranked, audited, and measured. Fixed-term faculty and researchers find themselves after years of study constantly living at the precipice. We cannot provide certainty in an uncertain world, but we need not manufacture insecurity.

As John Dewey (1929, 228) noted many years ago, "Long exposure to danger breeds an overpowering love of security. Love for security, translated into a desire not to be disturbed and unsettled, leads to dogmatism, to acceptance of beliefs upon authority." To avoid that, in both universities and research institutes as well as other domains of social life, we need to work to enact policies that promote security. Moreover, we need to do that differently in different locales. In some instances, it may involve a *reductio ad absurdum* of neoliberal policies. For example, one might participate only in activities that are rewarded in audits, neglecting other tasks. Alternatively, it may require refusing to go along with the practices that promote insecurity in the name of efficiency. It may involve electing politicians who will fight to promote policies that establish greater security for faculty, students, and staff.

In short, enhancing security involves continuously rebalancing what Isaiah Berlin (1969) called positive freedoms, those freedoms that allow each of us to be the masters of our own fate, with negative freedoms, those that allow us to act without being blocked by others. Franklin D. Roosevelt expressed this well (using somewhat different categories) when he proposed four freedoms: freedom of speech and religion, freedom from want and hunger. Neoliberals have stressed the importance of positive freedoms such as freedom of speech and religion while ignoring the importance of negative freedoms such as freedom from want and hunger. Clearly, without adequate freedom from want and hunger, freedom of speech and religion are nearly meaningless. Conversely, freedom from want and hunger without freedom of speech and religion effectively block our liberties.

But we also need to extend these freedoms. We need to demand that everyone have sufficient freedom from want that, if they so desire, they can pursue higher education, develop their capacities individually and collectively to the fullest, and overcome the limitations imposed by poverty and want. Moreover, we need to do this in a manner that emphasizes that so doing is not merely an *individual* good, but a *social* good, especially if we are to enhance democracy while addressing the crises that confront us. We also need to ensure that scholars in universities and research institutes have sufficient liberties that they can pursue their professions without fear of negative sanctions so that the dogmatism described by Dewey does not take root.

That is to say, we need to provide sufficient security such that universities and research institutes can reclaim their place as *learning communities*. Universities and research institutes are not and cannot survive as places where autonomous individuals with similar desires congregate. They must foster and maintain a sense of community. In particular, they must strive to become learning communities. Doing this will not be easy, but it is certainly not beyond our capabilities. Consider some of the things that we could do with relatively little effort:

1. We might reform or abolish the credit hour. The widely used credit hour system presumes that the best measure of student learning is the amount of time he or she spends in class staring at a faculty member, and that the best measure of the effort and quality provided in teaching is the amount of time a faculty member stands in front of the room. We all know that this is patently false. Yet the credit hour[1] has become *de facto* our means of measuring student and faculty performance. We could do far better by focusing on student learning outcomes and transforming lectures into dialogues as explained below.

2. We might reject most standardized testing. Standardized testing is a cheap, easily employed means by which we can measure

learning. Unfortunately, it often tends to measure the wrong things, including how good people are at taking standardized tests. It does an excellent job at measuring recall and simple problem solving (where the answer to the problem is well established). But it fails miserably at measuring creativity, critical thinking, or the ability to grasp important nuances that make the difference between understanding and rote memorization. It also fails to develop the ability to use knowledge to engage in practical actions. Hence, it is perhaps even counterproductive in the workplace, in family life, in politics, in science, and in making the difficult decisions that all of us face at one time or another.

Furthermore, most standardized testing is part of an outmoded and inadequate grading system. It reduces education to listening to a "sage on stage" who provides the facts to students. Yet in our fast-paced world, most of those facts will become irrelevant or erroneous soon after graduation. At worst, it promotes the notion that higher education is merely a means for obtaining the credentials necessary to obtain a job and increased income. We would do far better evaluating students based on competencies as demonstrated through practicums, journaling, exercises in critical thinking, and a variety of group projects that address issues beyond the classroom. In short, we would do better by focusing on learning outcomes— on what a student should be able to *do* as a result of a learning activity (see e.g., Bernholt, Neumann, and Nentwig 2012).

3. We might transform higher education by minimizing the use of classroom lectures and canned laboratory experiments. The classroom lecture and canned laboratory experiment (in which the "answer" is already known) were designed as means of allowing an apparently all-knowing professor to impart

knowledge to others. They have been a dismal failure on several grounds. It has been well known for years that most of what is said in lectures is forgotten soon afterward. Moreover, lectures employ a passive, unidirectional approach to learning in which knowledge is to be absorbed by students like a sponge absorbs water. Furthermore, lectures assume that knowledge is fixed, unchanging, and removed from the knower. In addition, lecturing erroneously assumes that knowledge does not pass from students to professors or among students. I, for one, find that it is precisely the naïve questions asked by students that challenge what I thought I knew. I find that my students learn more when they engage in discussion with others.

4. We might use information technologies to tear down the walls between the classroom and the rest of the world. Today, we have the luxury of vast amounts of educational materials available on the web. This includes lectures of varying lengths, written and multimedia materials, as well as videos on an enormous range of subjects and a growing number of interactive websites. Moreover, with little effort, anyone with relatively minimal equipment can add to this vast collection. What this means is that we can now use informatics to invert and vastly improve the usual lecture-discussion format. Instead of having students come to class to listen to a lecture and discuss it among themselves afterward, we can ask them to listen to a lecture (or read some online texts, watch a visual presentation, listen to a podcast, or participate in an exercise) at their convenience and come to class prepared to discuss it. This can be supplemented by more traditional textbooks and other written materials. Similarly, we can develop laboratory and field experiments where the results are not already known, where students can

learn not only about the world but about how scholars go about querying and improving our understandings of the world.

Doing this will require making much of the process of education into group projects. In point of fact, nearly all our students find themselves in group activities of one sort or another after graduation. Ironically, many of the world's top companies often make group activities central to their operation. Yet we tend to treat education as if it were an entirely individualized (and individualizing) activity. Once we agree to create learning communities, we open the door to group projects of all sorts. Group projects offer the potential for group discovery as well as provide opportunities to learn how to work with persons one hardly knows, who disagree with you, and who—in some instances— are even obnoxious.

**Make universities and research institutes into models of democracy, deliberation, and discourse.** In their efforts to bring the freedoms of the market world into being, neoliberals have through New Public Management, the Human Capital theory of education, and related changes imposed on everyone new forms of discipline based on various forms of hierarchical control. In contrast, we need a world in which multiple worlds are constantly in play (Boltanski and Thévenot 2006 [1991]). We need a world in which the civic, environmental, industrial, inspirational, opinion, domestic, and other orders of worth are not subordinate to the market order, but in which there is an ongoing discourse about promoting, (re)constructing, and (re) imagining multiple orders of worth. *We need to challenge the commonplace view that hierarchies are the only way—perhaps the best way—to organize all organizations.* After all, the persons and things that dwell in democracies and emerge from universities and research institutes—students, faculty, research results, and new understandings of the world—are not well suited to norms of hierarchy and mass production.[2]

In contrast, we would do well to pursue *heterarchy*, a term coined by neurologist Warren McColloch (1945). As David Stark (2009) has cogently illustrated through fieldwork in a variety of organizations, heterarchy may be understood as self-organization. It can be contrasted with the top-down organization of hierarchy. Importantly, hierarchies tend to be linked to singular orders of worth, singular means of evaluation, and singular chains of command. In contrast, heterarchies are places where multiple orders of worth are discussed and debated, and where organizational goals are understood to be in flux in response to a rapidly changing organizational environment. This is the case because new ideas, new means for enacting those ideas and citizens competent for life in a democracy, emerge from discourse and deliberation. They emerge from reflection on taken-for-granted notions about the way things are. They emerge from the design, debate, and implementation of imagined futures. In point of fact, as Stark notes, many of the most dynamic companies have at least partially abandoned hierarchies in favor of heterarchies.

Hence, we need to burst the neoliberal bubble so well formulated by the late Margaret Thatcher as "There Is No Alternative" (TINA). We need to show that the emperor has no clothes. We need to imagine a host of alternative futures. We need to demand that our political parties challenge the existing neoliberal hegemony by illustrating the existence of alternatives (even within the existing neoliberalisms) (e.g., Gibson-Graham 2006) and performing experiments designed to construct alternatives.

This will not be easy because the implementation of New Public Management creates a decline in collegiality and a rise of managerial control. "In normative terms, managerialism represents a distinctive discourse based upon a set of values that justify the assumed right of one group to monitor and control the activities of others" (Kolsaker 2008, 515). However, that control is never complete; in fact it depends in part on the willing participation of those who are controlled.

Clearly, the challenge here is to develop means of democratic deliberation and discourse that take into account the different situations, competencies, and abilities of different persons. But this is hardly radically different from the (re)building of democracies in nation-states. What is essential here is to avoid simply deciding *ex ante* what democracy is and attempting to implement it. Instead, we need to begin by asking: What do we mean by democracy? What kinds of institutional structures would promote it best? Do our extant universities and research institutes meet those expectations, both in terms of internal governance and preparation of future citizens? If not, how might we modify them so as to promote better democratic governance? Moreover, we need to resist the temptation to produce universal, permanent, unchanging answers to these questions. They need to be asked again and again in light of an ever-changing world.

**Help build more sustainable societies.** Universities and research institutes have their work cut out for them for at least the next century: helping to produce more sustainable societies. They can do this by defining what sustainability might be (an ongoing and never-finished task) and developing sociotechnical means for making human societies more sustainable. Moreover, sustainability is a wicked problem.

Consider the current enthusiasm for the "knowledge economy." Proponents suggest that knowledge is only needed to win
some imagined competition among nations. This is particularly
apparent in the so-called Bologna Process, which is designed to
standardize degrees throughout Europe. Alas, "... the most common feature of the Bologna Process documents is references
to the new global competitive order which compels European
nations to join forces in order to increase the 'attractiveness and
competitiveness of European higher education'..." (Christou
2010, 579). It is entirely unclear just what purpose this global
competition is to serve and what winning (or losing) might
mean. This is especially true as a small number of transnational
corporations dominate most major industries; these corporations have little or no incentive to be concerned about which
*nation* is winning or losing as long as their *corporation* is doing
well. In short, resolving the problems that confront us as human
beings is not merely a matter of amassing more and more facts
about science, engineering, and mathematics, thereby propel-
ling a given nation forward (toward what?) as some proponents
of the knowledge economy would have us believe. Nor is it
merely the integration of citizens into the labor market; indeed,
this is "Humboldt's nightmare" (Baillargeon 2011).

Instead, it requires that we build a global "*ecology of knowledge*" in which technoscientific knowledge is one form of knowledge among many. In this ecology of knowledge, local knowledge
about how everyday worlds are constructed, cultural knowledge
about how to act in the world, moral knowledge about what is
the right thing to do, and sociotechnical knowledge are explic-
itly recognized and even embraced as interacting.[3]

As suggested in a report recently commissioned by the
Directorate-General for Research of the European Commission,

"… all of the key reference points in science and governance are variously the objects of collective imagination: social priorities, purposes, and outcomes in steering research; misgivings concerning the directions, governance, and consequences of innovation; ethical issues in research and application; publics and their concerns and capacities; and expectations concerning social learning and adaptation to innovation" (Wynne et al. 2007, 11–12).

In the context of universities and research institutes, this means grappling with the wicked problems that concern us collectively involves moving beyond multidisciplinary projects, problems, and programs to interdisciplinary ones in which the knowledge of each discipline—obtained in continuous dialogue with practitioners—is constantly challenged and/or confirmed by knowledge emerging from other disciplines, and in which other knowledges, not found within universities and research institutes, are taken seriously.

Indeed, if we are to avoid becoming mere cogs in the neoliberal machine, we must abandon pursuing our hyperspecialized subdisciplinary interests independently of other knowledges. As scholars we must avoid the Scylla of independent hyperspecialization and the Charybdis of accepting all forms of knowledge as equal regardless of the situation. We must educate our next generation of scholars to relish that interaction.

In order to do this, the current passion for assessments of faculty, students, and staff must be the subject of intellectual debate. We must *assess assessment* (Nature 2010). Too often, administrators, caught up in enthusiasm over New Public Management, see any critique of assessments and audits as subversive (Lorenz 2012). Moreover, they often resist asking obvious questions: What degree of assessment is appropriate to the tasks at hand? Do the measures employed in the assessments actually measure what they claim to measure? What aspects of quality are excluded by the insistence on using quantitative indicators? Is the cost of management control less than the money saved by such control? Nor do they address an even more important issue with respect to universities: To what degree does excessive assessment undermine trust, thereby creating many of the problems noted above? As philosopher Onora O'Neill (2002, 52) poignantly notes, we must ask "... to whom the new audit culture makes professionals and institutions accountable, and for what it makes them accountable."

In contrast, what is sorely needed and should be demanded by scholars is that the process of assessment be opened to serious debate and analysis. We need to ask: What are the goals of assessments? What are the consequences—both financial and nonfinancial—of assessments? We need to debate how to minimize the negatives while promoting the positives. Doing so requires that faculty challenge the received wisdom in universities and research institutes in democratic nations that faculty deal with the intellectual matters while administrators deal with administrative matters. In point of fact, once one opens the black box of New Public Management, that distinction evaporates.

Yet it is also important to emphasize that this in no way is to suggest that we don't need administrators. Each university and research institute must have competent administrators who perform vital functions. What we must reject, however, is the notion that a hierarchical, corporate model of administration is appropriate to the university. It is increasingly problematic for the business world; accepting it in universities and research institutes is tantamount to abandoning the entire purpose of the university.

**Better integrate research and education.** Currently, at most universities, research is done with little or no input from undergraduates. Conversely, undergraduates rarely have an opportunity to engage in research themselves. Yet both research and education could benefit from such interactions. For example, Professor James Smith of my university teaches a biology course in which students work with popcorn to achieve a set of learning outcomes. The students review the primary scientific literature, design experiments, carry them out in the lab, and develop posters explaining their results.[4] In short, they learn biology by being engaged in research. Other scholars in other fields have developed similar projects and courses. In short, when students are emotionally engaged, when there is a link between the subject and their lives, when they grapple with complex problems and experiments, and when the focus is on learning outcomes rather than grades, students are most likely to learn (Stipek 2011).

**Recognize the importance of slow scholarship.** Recently, a group of German academics created the (virtual) Slow Science Academy. As they note on their website: "Science needs time to think. Science needs time to read, and time to fail. Science does not always know what it might be at right now. Science develops unsteadily, with jerky moves and unpredictable leaps forward—at the same time, however, it creeps about on a very slow time scale, for which there must be room and to which justice must be done" (Slow-Science.org 2010).

The only modification that I would suggest is that what they describe is true of all scholarship. We can use the Aristotelian definition of science as a system of knowledge, or we can substitute the word scholarship for science. Either way, we need to slow down to accomplish our (self-)assigned tasks.

This in no way suggests abandoning the now ubiquitous electronic networks that connect us with colleagues half a world away in a matter of nanoseconds. What it does mean is that valid research and scholarship emerge only when the time to think, reflect, read, and even fail are built into the very system of scholarship in which we live.

Furthermore, neither research nor education nor public engagement is a race. Although it is easier to pin down specifics than to make global generalizations, there is little question that pressure to produce at research universities and institutes has increased dramatically over the last 30 to 40 years. Scholars who are candidates for promotion often have more publications than the combined numbers of those who make up the promotion committee. Younger scholars are far less likely to engage in intellectual discussion with colleagues or a discussion over lunch if it is not directly related to a grant application or research project. Faculty spend less time in their offices (especially those who do not have laboratory obligations) because they need more uninterrupted time to engage in writing (Wilson 2010).

Yet the obsession with counting publications, citations, and other easily measured facets of faculty life is a poor means of judging the productivity or creativity of faculty members; it is even more problematic in judging their quality. Furthermore, it distorts scholarly publication in numerous ways as noted above. For the most part, scholars have tended to go along with this transformation or have compensated for it by dividing their research into small pieces, rarely suggesting alternatives.

A far better approach could be easily devised. For example, at appropriate times, one could ask the person to be reviewed to put forward his or her best four or five publications for review by colleagues (and perhaps by external reviewers) (West 2010). Such a review would have to be based on reading the papers rather than relying on scores obtained using various measures. It would discourage churning out poor quality research, and it would rely directly on the content of the publications. Moreover, because it would promote quality over quantity, it would also reduce the clutter that tends to fill up far too many academic journals.

**Bring the arts and humanities back in.** Although the sciences and engineering arose out of the arts and humanities half a millennium ago (Edgerton 2006; Romanyshyn 1989), the split between the humanities and sciences (beginning during the 19th century) has had the dual effect of disconnecting technoscience from the central questions that must be addressed in every society and allowing technical pathways to be determined largely by marketability. As Dominque Pestre (2007, 48) has argued, "… in technoscientific affairs, the first form of encounter and appropriation of a product is often outside of a dialogue because it is picked up by the market. Products are made available—and the confrontation of the product and its effects is made effective and is experienced before being debated. The technological novelty enters into the social, modifies social equilibria, displaces the actors—even before they begin to speak of it."

Moreover, the corporatization of the university has downgraded the arts and humanities (Donoghue 2010). We must bring the humanities back into the center of debates over education and technoscience. We must recognize that technologies and societies are co-produced (Jasanoff 2005; Latour 2011).

Furthermore, the arts and humanities have the potential to pose new questions, many of which can be addressed through the technosciences. We need not accept C. P. Snow's (1959) "Two Cultures" as some fixed and eternal barrier between cultural and scientific knowledge production. In fact, the sciences and engineering rely heavily on rhetoric (in the creation of scholarly journal articles and papers presented at professional meetings), on art (in the form of figures, graphs, charts, and illustrations of technical objects), on aesthetics (e.g., false color images in astronomy), and in determining the value (to human beings) of any technoscientific project. Similarly, the arts and humanities rely on technoscience for technical objects (paints, papers, ink, computers) and are always produced in concert with (or in a critique of) our increasingly technoscientific culture. In summary, the division between the arts and humanities and the technosciences is destructive of our shared values. We would do well to bring these two areas of human endeavor back together again.

**Teach each other and various publics.** We need to teach each other and various publics about the failures and dangers of neoliberalisms to democracy as well as to our future survival on the planet. As scholars we must transcend our narrow subdisciplinary specialties and converse with each other, our students, and various publics about both neoliberalisms' failures as well as urgent questions about democracies and threats to our future survival. This means that we must engage in research to better understand and develop alternatives to neoliberalisms.

Despite more than half a century of neoliberal developments, there is remarkably little scholarship on neoliberalisms and their transformation of the worlds in which we live. Moreover, far too much of the existing scholarship is arcane, addressing narrow scholarly communities, and unavailable to the general public. We can and must do better. We need simultaneously to (1) continue to connect and debate with our peers through our research, (2) make our research intelligible to various lay publics, and (3) take seriously the concerns raised by various publics. This has been possible in other domains such as the incorporation of activist groups into scientific debates over HIV/ AIDS (Epstein 1996). Surely it is possible to do so with respect to neoliberalisms.

**Perform differently.** Let us remember that the neoliberal world that is being built depends not solely on negative sanctions but on the positive participation in its construction by those of us who find (aspects of) it unacceptable. Performing differently, subversively if you wish, is a means for revealing both its constructed character as well as developing alternatives, of developing new settings that allow alternatives to come into being (Sarason 1972). As John Dewey suggested, experimenting is a fundamental part of the human experience. It is through experiment that we learn new ways of acting in the world. Of course, controlled experiments of the sort done in laboratories are hardly possible in most social settings. For a variety of ethical, logistical, and financial reasons, we cannot establish controlled experiments throughout society. But even controlled experiments illustrate the experimentality of the world. Hence, even after careful testing under a variety of conditions, pharmaceuticals, automobiles, financial instruments, children's toys, and food products are sometimes found wanting and recalled. By recognizing the experimentality of the world, we can begin to perform differently. We can focus on different means and ends— those that promote democracy and social justice and address the wicked problems of the 21st century.

Performing differently also means *forming alliances* and networks with other persons and groups concerned about the future of democracy. An obvious place to start here is through alliances with elementary and secondary school teachers. They have been far more disciplined by the neoliberal turn than we who work in higher education and research. Moreover, they are teaching those who will be first our future students and later our future leaders. They are to a much greater degree than universities under the increasing burden of New Public Management. In addition, they have been charged with instilling neoliberal values in the next generation as well as denying or obfuscating those values that do not fit within the neoliberal imagination.

Performing differently also means *changing our pedagogy*. It means showing our students and members of various publics the limits and threats to democracy of neoliberalisms. It means viewing neoliberalisms not merely as problems to be addressed but as pedagogical opportunities to be valued. It means bringing our concerns about academic freedom to the fore in our classes, laboratories, and research projects. Moreover, although some of these pedagogical changes can take place within our classrooms, offices, and laboratories, doubtless some will need to take place elsewhere.

We can also perform differently by *using marketing to propose and enact alternatives* to neoliberalism. This may appear to be a rather unusual and perhaps even undesirable approach. After all, marketing is intimately connected with the promotion of products and services for sale. But it is important to remember that there is nothing inherent in marketing skills that requires that they be used to promote goods and services. To the contrary, marketing can be and has been used to promote overtly political ends as well as a wide range of public goods. These include public goods such as threats to the environment, conservation of energy, and action on climate change. One particularly poignant example is the plebiscite held in Chile in 1988 that ended the dictatorial Pinochet regime. It was won in part by a marketing campaign that encouraged people to overcome their fears and vote "No." Such a campaign might also be used to unmask the shallowness of the current notion that education is solely about getting a job, as well as to promote concrete alternatives that resonate with various publics.

Additionally, although we certainly cannot count on the enthusiastic response of many wealthy individuals, foundations, and corporations as have the neoliberals, we can learn from their tactics. The neoliberals are not *laissez-faire* liberals; they are fully aware that the neoliberal world must be constructed (although they work hard to conceal that constructedness behind a curtain of naturalness). If we are to replace/modify/transform neoliberalisms, then we must simultaneously show how the contemporary world is constructed—with its emphasis on certain market freedoms, risk, recasting selves as social isolates—and use similar tactics to construct alternative futures. Moreover, we need to learn from the neoliberals the importance of acting on changes at various levels simultaneously. As the late James Buchanan (2009) suggested, we need to conceive, define, and enact (1) constitutional changes, (2) statutory changes, (3) institutional changes, (4) actions by private voluntary organizations, and (5) actions by individuals.

We must also remember that neoliberalisms are not monolithic. There is still considerable support, both within and outside the scholarly community, for equality and diversity, as well as for education and research as public goods. Even the European University Association, in the Gratz Declaration signed in Leuven in July 2003 felt it necessary to confirm that "Higher Education exists to serve the public interest and is not a 'commodity', a fact which WTO Member States recognized through

UNESCO and other international and multilateral bodies, conventions and declarations" (quoted in Lynch 2006, 10).

In addition, by virtue of the fact that neoliberalisms must be performed, they are somewhat different in each locale where they are enacted. Just as in the case of plays, concerts, and football games, there are good and bad, competent and incompetent, innovative and ritualistic performances of neoliberalism. Hence, there are always interstices where someone or some group can perform differently. We need to go one step further and use these interstices to develop and experiment with alternatives. In this endeavor, like the neoliberals, we are only fettered by our collective imaginations.

## Conclusion: Toward a Plural World

**The neoliberals were right in arguing that all knowledge is incomplete.** But the neoliberals failed to recognize two correlates of this insight. First, they failed to recognize that there are no exceptions to the rule of incompleteness (or if there are, there is no way for us to sort them out); mathematics—an extraordinarily useful set of tools—cannot provide an Archimedean point that will allow us to move the world. Second, they failed to recognize that the incompleteness of knowledge means that what *I* know is always insufficient for the reality of the world; it is by virtue of what *we* know that we gain confidence (but never certainty) about our knowledge of the world. Third, as useful as they are, markets provide at best a poor substitute for discourse.

Similarly, *the neoliberals were certainly right when they warned us of the dangers of totalitarian states and massive bureaucracies that impinge on human freedom.* Indeed, they warned us at a time when many in the scholarly community were celebrating the supposed superiority of the Soviet regime or the eugenics practiced by the Nazis. But we have also learned from the attempt to replace the State by the market. In particular, we have learned that there is no escape from governance. The withdrawal of the

State from certain aspects of governance merely opens the door for other forms. As social beings—between full autonomy and full sociality—we can never completely resolve the question of governance.

Indeed, from neoliberal perspectives, markets are about producing efficiencies and thereby maximizing wealth and liberty. But markets can also be about other values besides efficiency. It is precisely because markets may be designed to optimize or maximize many different values that they must be considered a form of governance rather than some naturally occurring or logically justifiable phenomenon.

In addition, the current neoliberal obsession with the market extends one order of worth to all human activities. Not only education, but technoscience, politics, family life, health care, citizenship, and social life in general are all reenacted in terms of autonomous rational economic actors operating in markets or market-like situations. Of particularly grave concern is that citizenship in a democratic society is undermined. "The privatised, consumer-led citizenry of the neoliberal model are reared on a culture of insecurity that induces anxiety, competition, and indifference to those more vulnerable than themselves" (Lynch 2006, 3).

Moreover, in rearranging the rewards and sanctions throughout society, the obsession with the market transforms both institutions and our very selves. We are told that we can succeed only if we act as entrepreneurial selves, turning all concerns into economic ones that can be resolved through market calculations. If we fail, then we are quickly told that this is the result of our personal failure to make the right choices or follow the appropriate rules.

Thus, even as neoliberals celebrate liberty, freedom, and choice, the institutions they build constrain our choices by developing elaborate rules for competitions and quasi-markets as well as choice architectures (Thaler and Sunstein 2008) in which choices are claimed to be merely apolitical technical matters. As such, other orders of worth beyond the market do not figure among the choices.

In higher education and research, the rules of organization and competition are usually only partially established by legislative bodies. More often, they are set by bureaucratic bodies that almost always operate at a distance from the institutions they regulate. These bureaucratic entities include both specialized government agencies that enforce New Public Management and the sometimes private entities that certify and accredit universities and research institutes. Similarly, violations of the rules are often adjudicated not by judicial bodies but the same bureaucratic bodies that establish the rules.

Thus, ultimately the audits, New Public Management, and neoliberal actions to colonize the world with quasi-markets and competitions are the mirror image of the Soviet State. Like State Socialism, they maintain a facade of popular participation, but they create their own *nomenklatura* who—behind the scenes— manipulate both the institutions over which they exercise authority and the individual selves subject to their jurisdiction. Like State Socialism, which created massive bureaucracies to govern virtually all activities through State action, neoliberalisms also create massive bureaucracies that govern all activities by imposing insecurity and risk on the entire population. Like State Socialism, which attempted through education and indoctrination to fashion selves only supportive of the State, neoliberalism attempts to fashion entrepreneurial selves that respond solely to the rules of the market. Like State Socialism, which funneled students into "priority" occupations such as engineering, neoliberalism funnels students into the STEM disciplines and business. Like State Socialism, which promoted the image of the productive worker, neoliberalism promotes the marketing and branding of everything and everyone.

Yet the solution to this problem is neither to banish markets nor banish States. It is to allow—indeed, encourage—multiple orders of worth to exist side by side. It is to understand that distribution may be based on market exchange but also on what people deserve or need. It is to recognize that we can build better, freer, more equal, more democratic societies. In the sphere of higher education, this means challenging the currently prevailing wisdom that education is all about getting a good job. It means ensuring that all students are exposed to a variety of (individual and social) images of the future. It means rejecting the insistence on limiting assessments to calculable outcomes in research and teaching, thereby rejecting standardization even as we accept standards. It means preparing each of us—students, faculty, and the general public—as well as our institutions of higher education and research to grapple with the multiple and intertwined crises that face all of us.

# Notes

### Preface to the English Language Edition

1. For my purposes here, I leave folk knowledge and self-knowledge to the side.

2. Of course, not all universities are research universities—universities that combine research and education (and often outreach) within their range of activities. The growing competition has tended to downgrade the value of the vast majority of universities that focus largely on teaching.

### Liberalism and Neoliberalisms

1. The historical roots of neoliberalism and its philosophical position(s) have been described elsewhere (e.g., Bourdieu 1998 [2007]; Foucault 2008; Harvey 2005).

2. Within economics this is known as the principal-agent problem. In brief, the problem is how to motivate an agent to act in the best interests of the principal and not in his or her own interests.

### Administration

1. There is considerable debate on this subject because the definition of who counts as an administrator varies from one campus to the next.

2. The Web of Science has changed names and owners several times. Other names include the Science Citation Index and the Institute for Scientific Information.

3. This is not to suggest that bureaucrats find themselves in a position of greater freedom than those they audit. To the contrary, in most instances they are subject to audit by other members of the bureaucracy. Indeed, even those at the top of the hierarchy find themselves bound by a set of increasingly formal rules and expectations.

4. For a review of several ranking systems, see Jöns and Hoyler (2013).

5. According to the survey document, this was recently added to the university's strategic plan. I doubt that many faculty members were familiar with the contents of that plan.

6. Martin and Ouellet (2010) report similar although more modest increases in salaries for top officials at Québec's universities.

7. Recently, the European Union developed U-multirank, which largely relies on data on a wide range of indicators provided by the universities. However, the project is in doubt for a variety of reasons (Rabesandratana 2013).

## Education

1. In contrast, Davidson College, a small, private liberal arts college with a large endowment relative to its size, decided to eliminate student loans and provide scholarships for those who could not afford its high tuition. The results have been startling: Not faced with high student loan debt to pay off, students are choosing occupational paths that involve community service rather than high salaries (Newsome 2012).

2. For a defense of foreign language instruction by a biologist, see Petsko (2010).

3. INSEAD does require a second language for applicants from English-speaking nations.

4. Martin and Ouellet (2010) make the same argument about higher education in Québec.

5. For the confessions of a ghost writer, see Dante (2010).

**Research**

1. The Web of Science as of February 3, 2013.

2. The former term derives from the receipt of a single sum for use at a particular research institute, whereas the latter term refers to the use of a formula for allocating funds by some State agency.

3. The problem has become sufficiently important that publishers have banded together to create CrossCheck, an organization that uses a computer program (iThenticate) to check submitted manuscripts for plagiarism.

4. The journal *Communications of the Association for Information Systems* (2009) found this action sufficiently widespread as to devote an entire issue to the subject.

**Consequences**

1. "The prospect of domination of the nation's scholars by Federal employment, project allocations, and the power of money is ever present and is gravely to be regarded" (Eisenhower 1961).

**Remembrance of Things Future**

1. In the United States, it was initially developed as part of a program to provide pensions to faculty members (Laitinen 2013).

2. Mass production is gradually disappearing from the industrialized world. Indeed, were it not for the existence of nations with cheap labor, it is likely that much mass production would now be entirely automated (Busch and Gunter 1995).

3. Even within highly specialized technoscientific worlds, multiple perspectives and enactments are commonplace (e.g., Anspach 1987).

4. For more details of Professor Smith's experiments, see: https://msu.edu/course/lb/494/s12/syllabus_s12.html. For another example, see Fukami (2013).

# References

AERES. 2013. *Rapports d'évaluation*. Agence d'évaluation de la recherche et de l'enseignment supérieure 2013 [cited May 2 2013]. Available from http://www.aeres-evaluation.com.

Akerlof, George A. 1970. The Market for "Lemons": Quality Uncertainty and the Market Mechanism. *Quarterly Journal of Economics* 84: 488–500.

Anderson, Janna Quitney, and Lee Rainie. 2012. *Millennials Will Benefit and Suffer Due to Their Hyperconnected Lives*. Washington, DC: Pew Research Center.

Anspach, Renee R. 1987. Prognostic Conflict in Life-and-Death Decisions: The Organization as an Ecology of Knowledge. *Journal of Health and Social Behavior* 28 (3): 215–231.

Apple, Michael W. 2006. *Educating the "Right" Way: Markets, Standards, God, and Inequality*. New York: Routledge.

Archambault, Éric, and Vincent Larivière. 2009. History of the Journal Impact Factor: Contingencies and Consequences. *Scientometrics* 79 (3): 635–649.

Arum, Richard, and Josipa Roksa. 2011. "Your So-Called Education." *The New York Times*, May 15, 10.

Atlas Economic Research Foundation. 2013. *Atlas Network*. Atlas Economic Research Foundation 2013 [cited May 2 2013]. Available from https://atlasnetwork.org/.

Baillargeon, Normand. 2011. *Je ne suis pas une PME: Plaidoyer pour une université publique*. Montreal: Les Editions Poètes de Brousse.

Barham, Bradford L., Jeremy D. Foltz, and Daniel L. Prager. 2014. Making Time for Science. *Research Policy* 43 (1): 21–31.

Barrow, Clyde W. 2010. The Rationality Crisis in US Higher Education. *New Political Science* 32 (3): 317–344.

Bartlett, Thomas. 2009. Cheating Goes Global as Essay Mills Multiply. *Chronicle of Higher Education* 55 (28): A1.

Bathe, Greville, and Dorothy Bathe. 1935. *Oliver Evans: A Chronicle of Early American Engineering*. Philadelphia: Historical Society of Pennsylvania.

Becker, Gary, and Guity Becker. 1997. *The Economics of Life: From Baseball to Affirmative Action to Immigration, How Real-World Issues Affect Our Everyday Life*. New York: McGraw Hill.

Bergstrom, Carl T. 2010. Use Ranking to Help Search. *Nature* 465:870.

Berlin, Isaiah. 1969. *Four Essays on Liberty*. Oxford: Oxford University Press.

Bernholt, Sascha, Knut Neumann, and Peter Nentwig. 2012. *Making It Tangible. Learning Outcomes in Science Education*. Münster: Waxmann Verlag.

Berrett, Dan. 2012. *All About the Money* [September 18, 2012]. Available from http://chronicle.com/article/All-About-the-Money/134422/.

Berthels, Nele, Gert Matthijs, and Geertrui Van Overwalle. 2011. Impact of Gene Patents on Diagnostic Testing: A New Patent Landscaping Method Applied to Spinocerebellar Ataxia. *European Journal of Human Genetics* 19 (11): 1114–1121.

Blumenstyk, Goldie. *Colleges Scramble to Avoid Violating Federal-Aid Limit*, April 2 2011. Available from http://chronicle.com/article/Colleges-Scramble-to-Avoid/126986/.

de Boer, Harry, and Ben Jongbloed. 2012. A Cross-National Comparison of Higher Education Markets in Western Europe. In *European Higher Education at the Crossroads*, edited by Adrian Curaj, Peter Scott, Lazăr Vlasceanu, and Lesley Wilson, 553–571. Dordrecht: Springer.

Boldrini, Marcello. 1972. *Scientific Truth and Statistical Method*. New York: Hafner.

Boltanski, Luc, and Laurent Thévenot. 2006. *On Justification: Economies of Worth*. Princeton: Princeton University Press. ( 1991).

Borgman, Christine L., and Jonathan Furner. 2002. Scholarly Communication and Bibliometrics. *Annual Review of Information Science & Technology* 36:3–72.

Boulton, Geoffrey. 2010. *University Rankings: Diversity, Excellence and the European Initiative*. Leuven: League of European Research Universities.

Bourdieu, Pierre. 2007. *The Essence of Neoliberalism*. Le Monde Diplomatique (English Edition) 1998 [cited November 4 2007]. Available from http://mondediplo.com/1998/12/08bourdieu.

Braun, Tibor. 2010. How to Improve the Use of Metrics. *Nature* 465:870.

Browne, John. *Securing a Sustainable Future for Higher Education: An Independent Review of Education Funding and Student Finance*, 12 October 2010. Available from https://www.gov.uk/government/publications/the-browne-report-higher-education-funding-and-student-finance.

Buchanan, James M. 2003. Public Choice: Politics Without Romance. *Public Choice* 19 (3): 13–18.

Buchanan, James M. 2009. Economists Have No Clothes. *Rationality, Markets, and Morals* 0:151–156.

Bunting, A. H. 1979. *Science and Technology for Human Needs, Rural Development, and the Relief of Poverty*. New York: International Agricultural Development Service.

Burgin, Angus. 2012. *The Great Persuasion: Reinventing Free Markets since the Depression*. Cambridge, MA: Harvard University Press.

Busch, Lawrence, and Valerie Gunter. 1995. Le Tiers Monde: Est-il encore nécessaire? Biotechnologie, robotique et fin de la Guerre froide. In *Les Sciences Hors l'Occident au XXème Siècle*, edited by Roland Waast, 41–61. Paris: ORSTOM éditions.

Campbell, Donald T. 1979. Assessing the Impact of Planned Social Change. *Evaluation and Program Planning* 2 (1): 67–90.

Carlson, Scott, and Goldie Blumenstyk. 2012. The False Promise of the Education Revolution. *The Chronicle of Higher Education*, December 21, A1, A4–A5.

Cassidy, John. 2009. *How Markets Fail. The Logic of Economic Calamities*. New York: Farrar, Strauss and Giroux.

Castoriadis, Cornelius. 1998. *The Imaginary Institution of Society*. Cambridge, MA: MIT Press.

Christou, Miranda. 2010. Education in Real Time: The Globalization of Synchronized Learning. *Current Sociology* 58 (4): 570–596.

The Chronicle of Higher Education. 2012. "Salaries of Public-College Presidents, 2011 Fiscal Year." Accessed: February 12, 2013. http://chronicle.com/article/Salaries-of-Public-College/131916/

Colquhoun, David. Publish-or-Perish: Peer Review and the Corruption of Science, *The Guardian*, 5 September 2011. Available from https://www.theguardian.com/science/2011/sep/05/publish-perish-peer-review-science.

Communications of the Association for Information Systems. 2009. *Communications of the Association for Information Systems*. Vol. 25.

Crane, Diana. 1972. *Invisible Colleges: Diffusion of Knowledge in Scientific Communities*. Chicago: University of Chicago Press.

Cremonini, Leon, Paul Benneworth, Hugh Dauncey, and Don F. Wester-heijden. 2013. Reconciling Republican "Egalité" and Global Excellence Values in French Higher Education. In *Institutionalization of World-Class University in Global Competition*, edited by Jung Cheol Shin and Barbara M. Kehm, 99–123. Dordrecht: Springer.

Dante, Ed. 2010. The Shadow Scholar: The Man Who Writes Your Students' Papers Tells His Story. *Chronicle of Higher Education* 57 (13). Available at http://chronicle.com/article/The-Shadow-Scholar/125329/.

Decker, Robert S., Leslie Wimsatt, Andrea G. Trice, and Joseph A. Konstan. 2007. *A Profile of Federal-Grant Administrative Burden Among Federal Demonstration Partnership Faculty*. Evanston, IL: Faculty Standing Committee of the Federal Demonstration Partnership.

Dewey, John. 1929. *The Quest for Certainty*. New York: G.P. Putnam's Sons.

Dewey, John. 1961. *Democracy and Education*. New York: The Macmillan Company.

Dewey, John. 1962. *The Child and the Curriculum and the School and Society*. Chicago: The University of Chicago Press.

Didegah, Fereshteh, and Ali Gazni. 2011. The Extent of Concentration in Journal Publishing. *Learned Publishing* 24 (4): 303–310.

Diels, Johan, Mario Cunha, Célia Manaia, Bernardo Sabugosa-Madeira, and Margarida Silva. 2011. Association of Financial or Professional Conflict of Interest to Research Outcomes on Health Risks or Nutritional Assessment Studies of Genetically Modified Products. *Food Policy* 36:197–203.

DOAJ. 2013. *Directory of Open Access Journals*. DOAJ 2013 [cited March 17, 2013]. Available from http://doaj.org.

Docherty, Thomas. 2012. Research by Numbers. *Index on Censorship* 41 (3): 46–55.

Donoghue, Frank. 2010. Can the Humanities Survive the 21st Century? *The Chronicle of Higher Education*, September 10, B4–B5.

Dwoskin, Elizabeth. 2012. Calculating a College Degree's True Value. *BusinessWeek*, December 24–January 6, 44–46.

Economic and Social Research Council. (n.d.). *Business Engagement*. London. *ESRC*.

Edgerton, Samuel Y. 2006. Brunelleschi's Mirror, Alberti's Window, and Galileo's "Perspective Tube." *Historia, Ciencias, Saude--Manguinhos* 13:151–179.

Edlin, Aaron S., and Daniel L. Rubinfeld. 2004. Exclusion or Efficient Pricing? The "Big Deal" Bundling of Academic Journals. *Antitrust Law Journal* 72:119–157.

Eisenhower, Dwight D. *Farewell Address* [Speech], January 17, 1961. Available from http://mcadams.posc.mu.edu/ike.htm.

Epstein, Steven. 1996. *Impure Science: AIDS, Activism, and the Politics of Knowledge*. Berkeley: University of California Press.

Fanelli, Daniele. 2011. Negative Results Are Disappearing From Most Disciplines and Countries. *Scientometrics* 88 (3): 1–14.

Fang, Ferric C., R. Grant Steen, and Arturo Casadevall. 2012. Misconduct Accounts for the Majority of Retracted Scientific Publications. *Proceedings of the National Academy of Sciences of the United States of America* 109:17028–17033.

Fink, L. Dee. 2003. *Creating Significant Learning Experiences*. San Francisco: Jossey-Bass.

Finlayson, Alan. 2010. *Britain, Greet the Age of Privatised Higher Education*. openDemocracy 2010 [cited December 9, 2010]. Available from https://www.opendemocracy.net.

Foucault, Michel. 2008. *The Birth of Biopolitics: Lectures at the Collège de France, 1978–79*. New York: Palgrave Macmillan.

Franzoni, Chiara, Giuseppe Scellato, and Paula Stephan. 2011. Changing Incentives to Publish. *Science* 333:702–703.

Friedman, Milton. 2002. *Capitalism and Freedom*. Chicago: University of Chicago Press.

Fuglie, Keith, Paul Heisey, John King, Carl E. Pray, and David Schimmelpfennig. 2012. The Contribution of Private Industry to Agricultural Innovation. *Science* 338:1031–1032.

Fukami, Tadashi. 2013. Integrating Inquiry-Based Teaching with Faculty Research. *Science* 339:1536–1537.

Funtowicz, Silvio O., and Jerome R. Ravetz. 1993. Science for the Post-Normal Age. *Futures (London)* 25 (7): 739–755.

Gibson-Graham, J. K. 2006. *A Postcapitalist Politics*. Minneapolis: University of Minnesota Press.

Gingras, Yves. 2008. *La fièvre de l'évaluation de la recherche. Du mauvais usage de faux indicateurs*. Montreal: Centre Universitaire de Recherche sur la Science et al Technologie, Université du Québec à Montréal.

Giroux, Henry A. 2013. *The Politics of Disimagination and the Pathologies of Power* 2013 [cited March 3, 2013]. Available from http://www.truth-out.org/news/item/14814-the-politics-of-disimagination-and-the-pathologies-of-power.

Gori, Roland, and Marie-José Del Volgo. 2009. L'idéologie de l'évaluation: Un nouveau dispositif de servitude volontaire? *Nouvelle Revue de Psychosociologie* 2 (8): 11–26.

Government Accountability Office. 2011. *Postsecondary Education: Student Outcomes Vary at For-Profit, Nonprofit, and Public Schools*. Washington, DC: Government Accountability Office.

Greene, Jay P., Brian Kisida, and Jonathan Mills. 2010. *Administrative Bloat at American Universities: The Real Reason for High Costs in Higher Education*. Phoenix: Goldwater Institute.

Gusterson, Hugh. 2012. Want to Change Academic Publishing? Just Say No. *The Chronicle of Higher Education*, September 28, A26.

Hanafi, Sari. 2011. University Systems in the Arab East: Publish Globally and Perish Locally vs Publish Locally and Perish Globally. *Current Sociology* 59 (3): 291–309.

Harvey, David. 2005. *A Brief History of Neoliberalism*. Oxford: Oxford University Press.

Harwood, Jonathan. 2012. *Europe's Green Revolution: The Rise and Fall of Peasant-friendly Plant Breeding, Routledge Explorations in Economic History.* New York: Routledge.

Hayek, Friedrich August. 1943. The Facts of the Social Sciences. *Ethics* 54 (1): 1–13.

Hayek, Friedrich August. 1973–1979. *Law, Legislation and Liberty.* Chicago: University of Chicago Press, 3 vols.

Hayek, Friedrich August. 1976. *The Mirage of Social Justice, Law, Legislation and Liberty.* Chicago: University of Chicago Press.

Hayek, Friedrich August. 2007. *The Road to Serfdom.* Chicago: University of Chicago Press.

Hechinger, John. 2012. The Troubling Dean-to-Professor Ratio. *BusinessWeek*, November 26, 40, 42.

Heller, Michael A., and Rebecca S. Eisenberg. 1998. Can Patents Deter Innovation? The Anticommons in Biomedical Research. *Science* 280 (5364): 698–701.

Hobbes, Thomas. 1651. *Leviathan.* London: Andrew Crooke.

Horn, Rob Van, and Philip Mirowski. 2009. The Rise of the Chicago School of Economics and the Birth of Neoliberalism. In *The Road from Mont Pèlerin: The Making of the Neoliberal Thought Collective*, edited by Philip Mirowski and Dieter Plehwe, 139–178. Cambridge, MA: Harvard University Press.

Hossein, Naomi, Richard King, and Alexandra Kelbert. 2013. Squeezed: Life in a Time of Food Price Volatility, Year 1 Results. In *Oxfam Research Reports*, edited by Oxfam. Oxford: Oxfam.

Houry, Debra. 2013. College Rankings: a Guide to Nowhere. *The Chronicle of Higher Education*, February 1, A56.

Huffman, Wallace, and Robert Evenson. 2006. Do Formula or Competitive Grant Funds Have Greater Impacts on State Agricultural Productivity? *American Journal of Agricultural Economics* 88 (4): 783–798.

Hwang, Woo Suk, Young June Ryu, Jong Hyuk Park, Eul Soon Park, Eu Gene Lee, Ja Min Koo, Hyun Yong Jeon, et al. 2004. Evidence of a Pluripotent Human Embryonic Stem Cell Line Derived from a Cloned Blastocyst. *Science* 303 (5664): 1669–1674.

Hyde, Abbey, Marie Clarke, and Jonathan Drennan. 2013. The Changing Role of Academics and the Rise of Managerialism. In *The Academic Profession in Europe: New Tasks and New Challenges*, edited by Barbara M. Kehm and Ulrich Teichler, 39–52. Dordrecht, the Netherlands: Springer.

INSEAD. 2013. *The Business School for the World*. INSEAD 2013 [cited March 17, 2013]. Available from http://www.insead.edu/home/.

Jacob, Brian, Brian McCall, and Kevin M. Stange. 2013. *College as Country Club: Do Colleges Cater to Students' Preferences for Consumption?* Washington, DC: National Bureau of Economic Research, Working Paper Series.

Jasanoff, Sheila. 2005. *Designs on Nature: Science and Democracy in Europe and the United States*. Princeton: Princeton University Press.

Jöns, Heike, and Michael Hoyler. 2013. Global Geographies of Higher Education: The Perspective of World University Rankings. *Geoforum* 46 (May): 45–69.

Kapeller, Jakob. 2010. Some Critical Notes on Citation Metrics and Heterodox Economics. *Review of Radical Political Economics* 42 (3): 330–337.

Katz, Stanley N. 2012. Beware Big Donors. *The Chronicle of Higher Education*, March 30, B5–B9.

Kehm, Barbara M., and Liudvika Leiðytë. 2010. Effects of New Governance on Research in the Humanities—The Example of Medieval History. In *Governance and Performance in the German Public Research Sector: Disciplinary Differences*, edited by Dorothea Jansen, 73–90. Dordrecht, the Netherlands: Springer.

Klein, Naomi. 2007. *The Shock Doctrine: The Rise of Disaster Capitalism*. New York: Picador.

Knorr-Cetina, Karin. 1981. *The Manufacture of Knowledge*. Oxford: Pergammon Press.

Kolsaker, Ailsa. 2008. Academic Professionalism in the Managerialist Era: A Study of English Universities. *Studies in Higher Education* 33 (5): 513–525.

Kuhn, Thomas. 1970. *The Structure of Scientific Revolutions*. Chicago: University of Chicago Press.

Kumar, M. 2010. The Import of the Impact Factor: Fallacies of Citation-Dependent Scientometry. *Bulletin of the Royal College of Surgeons of England* 92 (1): 26–30.

Langley, Paul. 2007. Uncertain Subjects of Anglo-American Financialization. *Cultural Critique* 65 (Winter): 67–91.

Laitinen, Amy. 2013. The Curious Birth and Harmful Legacy of the Credit Hour. *Chronicle of Higher Education* 59 (20): A23–A24.

Lashzone. 2013. *How Does It Work?* 2013 [cited February 3, 2013]. Available from http://www.lashzone.com/.

Latour, Bruno. 2005. *Reassembling the Social: An Introduction to Actor-Network-Theory*. Oxford: Oxford University Press.

Latour, Bruno. 2011. From Multiculturalism to Multinaturalism; What Rules of Method for the New Socio-Scientific Experiments? *Nature and Culture* 6 (1): 1–17.

Lave, Rebecca, Martin Doyle, and Morgan Robertson. 2010. Privatizing stream restoration in the US. *Social Studies of Science* 40 (5): 677–703.

Lave, Rebecca, Philip Mirowski, and Samuel Randalls. 2010. Introduction: STS and Neoliberal Science. *Social Studies of Science* 40 (5): 659–675.

Leshner, Alan I., and Steven J. Fluharty. 2012. Time and Money Are Being Wasted in the Lab. *The Chronicle of Higher Education*, December 7, A17.

Levinson, Marc. 2006. *The Box: How the Shipping Container Made the World Smaller and the World Economy Bigger.* Princeton: Princeton University Press.

Lippmann, Walter. 1938. *The Good Society.* London: George Allen And Unwin Ltd.

Lorenz, Chris. 2012. If You're So Smart, Why Are You under Surveillance? Universities, Neoliberalism, and New Public Management. *Critical Inquiry* 38 (3): 599–629.

Louis, Meera. 2013. Entrepreneurs on Hold. *BusinessWeek*, June 24–30, 54, 56.

Lynch, Kathleen. 2006. Neo-liberalism and Marketisation: The Implications for Higher Education. *European Educational Research Journal* 5 (1): 1–17.

Maher, Brendan. 2010. Sabotage! *Nature* 467:516–518.

Marginson, Simon. 2011. The New World Order in Higher Education. In *Questioning Excellence in Higher Education*, edited by Michele Rostan and Massimiliano Vaira, 3–20. Rotterdam: SensePublishers.

Markoff, John. 2013. "New Test for Computers: Grading Essays at College Level." *New York Times*, April 4, A1.

Martin, Eric, and Maxime Ouellet. 2010. *La gouvernance des universités dans l'économie du savoir.* Montréal: Institut de recherche et d'informations socio-économiques.

Mccafferty, Patricia. 2010. Forging a "Neoliberal pedagogy": The "Enterprising Education" Agenda in Schools. *Critical Social Policy* 30:541–563.

McCulloch, Warren S. 1945. The Heterarchy of Values Determined by the Topology of Nervous Nets. *Bulletin of Mathematical Biophysics* 7 (2): 89–93.

Mead, George Herbert. 1913. The Social Self. *Journal of Philosophy, Psychology, and Scientific Methods* 10 (January–December): 374–380.

Merrill, Stephen A., and Anne-Marie Mazza. 2010. *Managing University Intellectual Property in the Public Interest*. Washington, DC: The National Academy Press.

Merton, Robert K. 1968. The Matthew Effect in Science. *Science* 159 (3810): 56–63.

Mervis, Jeffrey. 2013. Expert Firms Play a Hidden Role in Connecting Science and Finance. *Science* 339:137–139.

Metcalf, Allan. 2013. In English, Anarchy Rules. *The Chronicle of Higher Education*, March 22, B2.

Mirowski, Philip. 2009. Postface. In *The Road from Mont Pèlerin: The Making of the Neoliberal Thought Collective*, edited by Philip Mirowski and Dieter Plehwe, 417–455. Cambridge, MA: Harvard University Press.

Mirowski, Philip. 2011. *Science-mart: Privatizing American Science*. Cambridge, MA: Harvard University Press.

Moe, Michael T., Kathleen Bailey, and Rhoda Lau. 1999. *The Book of Knowledge: Investing in the Growing Education and Training Industry*. New York: Merrill Lynch & Co.

Mok, Ka Ho. 2011. Regional Cooperation or Competition? The Rise of Transnational Higher Education and the Emergence of Regulatory Regionalism in Asia. 2011 Senior Seminar co-hosted by the East-West Center, UNESCO Bangkok, and Hong Kong Institute for Education. Bangkok.

Molotch, Harvey. 1976. The City as a Growth Machine: Toward a Political Economy of Place. *American Journal of Sociology* 82 (September): 309–332.

Mont Pelerin Society. 2009. *The Mont Pelerin Society* 2009 [cited March 18, 2009]. Available from https://www.montpelerin.org/.

Mytelka, Andrew. *Whistle-Blower Alleges That For-Profit College Paid Incentives to Student Recruiters*, May 7, 2010. Available from http://chronicle.com/blogs/ticker/whistle-blower-alleges-that-for-profit-college-paid-incentives-to-student-recruiters/23812.

National Survey of Student Engagement. 2012. *Promoting Student Learning and Institutional Improvement: Lessons from NSSE at 13*. Bloomington, IN: Indiana University Center for Postsecondary Research.

Nature. 2010. Assessing Assessment. *Nature* 465 (7300):845.

Newcastle University. 2013. "The Idea of a World-Class Civic University." Newcastle?: Newcastle University (advertising supplement to the Chronicle of Higher Education).

Newsome, Melba. 2012. The Debt-Free College Degree. *BusinessWeek*, September 10–16, 70–71.

O'Neill, Onora. 2002. *A Question of Trust*. Cambridge: Cambridge University Press.

Oreskes, Naomi, and Erik M. Conway. 2010. *Merchants of Doubt: How a Handful of Scientists Obscured the Truth on Issues from Tobacco Smoke to Global Warming*. New York: Bloomsbury Press.

Paasi, A. 2005. Globalisation, Academic Capitalism, and the Uneven Geographies of International Journal Publishing Spaces. *Environment & Planning A* 37 (5): 769–789.

Parry, Marc. 2012. Degrees, Designed by the Numbers. *The Chronicle of Higher Education*, August 3, A1, A4–A8.

Peekhaus, Wilhelm. 2010. The Neoliberal University and Agricultural Biotechnology: Reports From the Field. *Bulletin of Science, Technology & Society* 30 (6): 415–429.

Pestre, Dominique. 2007. La gouvernance des sciences en société, la gouvernance des sociétés en science: Les tensions entre savoirs, pouvoirs et démocratie. In *Sciences en société au XXIe siècle: Autres relations, autres pratiques*, edited by Jean-Pierre Alix, Bernard Ancori, and Pierre Petit, 41–51. Paris: CNRS Editions.

Petsko, Gregory A. 2010. A Faustian bargain. *Genome Biology* 11 (138): 1–3.

Pollack, Andrew. 2009. "Crop Scientists Say Biotechnology Seed Companies Are Thwarting Research." *The New York Times*, February 20, B3.

Proctor, Robert, and Londa L. Schiebinger. 2008. *Agnotology: The Making and Unmaking of Ignorance*. Stanford, CA: Stanford University Press.

Rabesandratana, Tania. 2013. "Brussels Ranking" of Universities off to a Rocky Start. *Science* 339 (6118): 383.

Rasmussen, David M. 1973. Between Autonomy and Sociality. *Cultural Hermeneutics* 1 (1): 3–45.

Rittel, Hörst W. J., and Melvin M. Webber. 1973. Dilemmas in a General Theory of Planning. *Policy Sciences* 4 (2): 155–169.

Rockwell, Sara. 2009. The FDP Faculty Burden Survey. *Research Management Review* 16 (2): 29–42.

Romanyshyn, Robert D. 1989. *Technology as Symptom and Dream*. New York: Routledge.

Rose, Nikolas, and Peter Miller. 1992. Political Power beyond the State: Problematics of Government. *British Journal of Sociology* 43 (2): 173–205.

Rougier, Louis. 1939a. "Allocution du Professor Louis Rougier." In *Le Colloque Walter Lippmann*, edited by Travaux du Centre International d'Etudes Pour la Rénovation du Libéralisme, 13–20. Paris: Librairie de Médicis, Cahier 1.

Rougier, Louis. 1939b. "Avant-propos." In *Le Colloque Walter Lippmann*, edited by Travaux du Centre International d'Etudes Pour la Rénovation du Libéralisme, 7–8. Paris: Librairie de Médicis, Cahier 1.

Rudy, Alan P., Dawn Coppin, Jason Konefal, Brad T. Shaw, Toby Ten Eyck, Craig Harris, and Lawrence Busch. 2007. *Universities in the Age of Corporate Science: The UC Berkeley-Novartis Controversy* . Philadelphia: Temple University Press.

Russell, H. L. 1931. *Commercial Support for Agricultural Research*. Paper read at Proceedings 45th Annual Convention of the Land Grant Colleges and Universities, Chicago, IL.

Sander, Libby. 2012. Economy Affects Students' Academic Performance as Well as Spending Decisions. *The Chronicle of Higher Education*, November 23, A11–A12.

Sappington, Thomas W., Kenneth R. Ostlie, Christina DiFonzo, Bruce E. Hibbard, Christian H. Krupke, Patrick Porter, Steven Pueppke, Elson J. Shields, and Jon J. Tollefson. 2010. Conducting Public-Sector Research on Commercialized Transgenic Seed: In Search of a Paradigm That Works. *GM Crops* 1 (2): 55–58.

Sarason, Seymour B. 1972. *The Creation of Settings and the Future Societies.* San Francisco: Jossey-Bass.

Schlatter, Richard. 1951. *Private Property: History of an Idea.* London: Allen and Unwin.

Schubert, Torben, and Ulrich Schmoch. 2010. New Public Management in Science and Incentive-Compatible Resource-Allocation Based on Indicators. In *Governance and Performance in the German Public Research Sector: Disciplinary Differences,* edited by Dorothea Jansen, 3–18. Dordrecht, the Netherlands: Springer.

Simon, Stephanie, and Stephanie Banchero. 2010. "Putting a Price on Professors." *Wall Street Journal,* October 23, C1.

Simons, Henry C. 1948 [1934]. A Positive Program for Laissez Faire: Some Proposals for a Liberal Economic Policy. In *Economic Policy for a Free Society,* 40–77. Chicago: University of Chicago Press.

Slow-Science.org. 2010. *The Slow Science Manifesto.* Slow Science Academy [cited February 13, 2013]. Available from http://slow-science.org/.

Snow, C. P. 1959. *The Two Cultures and the Scientific Revolution.* New York: Cambridge University Press.

Stark, David. 2009. *The Sense of Dissonance: Accounts of Worth in Economic Life.* Princeton: Princeton University Press.

Steneck, Nicholas H. 2013. Global Research Integrity Training. *Science* 340 (6132): 552–553.

Stipek, Deborah. 2011. Education Is Not a Race. *Science* 332: 1481.

Stutz, Bruce. 2010. Companies Put Restrictions on Research into GM Crops. *Environment 360: Opinion, Analysis, Reporting & Debate,* February

3, 2013. Available from http://e360.yale.edu/feature/companies_put
_restrictions_on_research_into_gm_crops/2273/.

Thaler, Richard H., and Cass R. Sunstein. 2008. *Nudge: Improving Decisions about Health, Wealth and Happiness*. London: Penguin.

The Chronicle of Higher Education. 2011. *Almanac of Higher Education*, March 26, 2014. Available from http://chronicle.com/article/How-Much -Presidential-Pay-Has/133391/.

 The Chronicle of Higher Education. 2013. *Salaries of Public-College Presidents, 2011 Fiscal Year* 2012 [cited February 12, 2013]. Available from http://chronicle.com/article/Salaries-of-Public-College/131916/.

Thévenot, Laurent. 2006. *L'Action au Pluriel: Sociologie des Régimes d'Engagement*. Paris: La Découverte.

Times Higher Education Supplement. 2010. *THE World University Rankings*, September 16, 2010 [cited April 22, 2012]. Available from https:// www.timeshighereducation.co.uk/world-university-rankings/.

Troop, Don. 2013. The Student Body, For Sale. *The Chronicle of Higher Education*, February 22, A16–A19.

van Noorden, Richard. 2010. A Profusion of Measures. *Nature* 465: 864–866.

Walzer, Michael. 1983. *Spheres of Justice: A Defense of Pluralism and Equality*. New York: Basic Books.

Warner, Keith D., Kent M. Daane, Christina M. Getz, Stephen P. Maurano, Sandra Calderon, and Kathleen A. Powers. 2011. The Decline of Public Interest Agricultural Science and the Dubious Future of Crop Biological Control in California. *Agriculture and Human Values* 28 (4): 483–496.

Warren, Cat, and Marion Nestle. 2010. Big Food, Big Agra, and the Research University [Interview with Marion Nestle]. *Academe Online*. Available from https://www.aaup.org/article/big-food-big-agra-and-research -university.

Washington Times. 2012. "The student debt explosion; Higher education bubble threatens to add to nation's economic woes." *The Washington Times*, December 6, 2.

Weigel, David. 2013. *The Republican War on Social Science*. Slate 2013 [cited April 30, 2013]. Available from http://www.slate.com/.

Wellings, Paul. 2010. Message from the Vice-Chancellor. Lancaster University, September 22.

West, Jevin D. 2010. Learn from Game Theory. *Nature* 465: 871–872.

Wilson, Robin. 2010. The Ivory Sweatshop: Academe Is No Longer a Convivial Refuge. *The Chronicle of Higher Education*, July 30, B28–B29.

Wislar, Joseph S., Annette Flanagin, Phil B. Fontanarosa, and Catherine D. DeAngelis. 2011. Honorary and Ghost Authorship in High Impact Biomedical Journals: A Cross Sectional Survey. *British Medical Journal* 343: 1–7.

Woodruff, Sarah B. 2013. *MSU Faculty Work Environment Survey Spring 2013*. Miami, OH: Ohio's Evaluation and Assessment Center.

Wynne, Brian, Michel Callon, Maria Eduarda Gonçalves, Sheila Jasanoff, Maria Jepsen, Pierre-Benoît Joly, Zdenek Konopasek, et al. 2007. *Taking European Knowledge Society Seriously*. Brussels: Directorate-General for Research.